Dairygo
Homes of Good Food

For you, from Ireland's top chefs,
all you need to recreate in your own home the
sumptuous menus enjoyed in the restaurants of
famous Irish Country Houses.

"Extremely good - sinful but delicious." Lord Henry
Mountcharles at Longueville

"This is my idea of paradise." Finbarr Wright at Marlfield

"A work of art." Phil Coulter at Rathsallagh

*"Mouthwatering, scrumptious. I must say I do like
traditional food."* Gillian Bowler at Ballymaloe

"We had a wonderful meal." Jennifer Johnston at
Hilton Park

*"The best of produce beautifully prepared and
served."* Paddy Cole at Newport House

Just some of the reactions of Bibi's fellow diners
during the TV series.

First published 1992 by O'Brien Press Ltd., 20 Victoria Road,
Rathgar, Dublin 6 and
Dairygold Food Products, Marian House,
New Square, Mitchelstown, Co. Cork.

ISBN 0-86278-303-8

Concept and editorial development by U.S.C.C. Ireland.
Design by Renaissance
Photographs by John Searle
Typeset at The O'Brien Press
Printing: Colour Books Ltd, Dublin

Dairygold
HOMES OF
GOOD FOOD

INTRODUCED BY
BIBI BASKIN

CONCEPT AND EDITORIAL DEVELOPMENT
U.S.C.C. Ireland Ltd

FOOD CONSULTANT
ALIX GARDNER
EDITORIAL ADVISOR
JOHN COLCLOUGH

THE O'BRIEN PRESS
DUBLIN

CONTENTS

Longueville House 60

Ballymaloe House 86

Menu 1 Quail stuffed with Chicken Mousseline
with a Tarragon Sauce 101
Carrot and Coriander Soup 102
Wild Salmon with Sorrel Sauce 103
Pineapple and Strawberry Timbale 104

Menu 2 Quenelles of Salmon, Turbot and Monkfish
with Carrot and Lime Sauce 105
Green Salad with Walnut Oil Dressing 107
John Dory with Potato Crust and
Champagne Sauce 108
Summer Pudding 109

Menu 3 Rillette of Duck 110
Leek and Potato Soup 111
Medallions of Venison with
Wild Mushroom and Game Sauce 111
Bread and Butter Pudding
with Whiskey Sauce 112

INTRODUCTION

Bibi Baskin

An old Chinese man who was a wonderful cook once said to me that God sends meat and the devil sends cooks. Once again the born sceptic in me finds ready fodder. Because the devil certainly did not send cooks to the Dairygold Homes of Good Food. Or if he did, they lost their way up the marvellous winding drives that front so many of these historic homes of haute cuisine.

Filming the Dairygold Homes of Good Food was not so much a labour of love as a hedonistic pursuit of excellence. It was duly rewarded. Among the six selected houses we found a cocktail of superior food, sinful luxury, a sense of history and above all a very authentic céad míle fáilte. All told the hallmark of the emergence of a new standard of Irish Country House cuisine, the equal of any of our European neighbours. This standard is well represented in our "Dairygold Homes of Good Food" recipes. The recipes celebrate the best of traditional Irish cooking, the rich bounty of our farms, seas and rivers, and cooking techniques from Cordon Bleu to Nouvelle.

Each Dairygold Home of Good Food tells a very distinctive story. The O'Callaghan family from Longueville House, in Co. Cork, originally the owners of a nearby castle before Cromwell invited them to Connaught, are now reinstated in the stately grandeur of Longueville once more. Contrast this with Hilton Park in Co. Monaghan, which has been home to eight generations of the Madden family.

Then there is the enterprise at Ballymaloe House, also in Co. Cork, where an original farmhouse has expanded to include a country house hotel, a cookery school, a craft shop and a restaurant.

On the other hand Newport House in Co. Mayo is a quiet operation. So silent that one of its most frequent visitors, the mayfly, has developed quite a following of regular angler-visitors.

Marlfield House in Co. Wexford brings its visitors back into the heart of the Regency period, and in recreating that stylish era provides a rare *degree of sumptuous luxury in the house which was once the dower house of the Earls of Courtown.*

In Rathsallagh House, Co. Wicklow, Kay and Joe O'Flynn have developed the stables into an hotel and their family home, where this farmer-turned-hotelier and his wife are centre stage to every guest's visit, a personalised round the clock role which frequently finishes with Joe as master of ceremonies around the piano late into the night.

Whatever your own choice of country house may be, the Dairygold Homes of Good Food, without exception, will guarantee you a memorable experience of the excellence of Irish cuisine and the conviviality of Irish hospitality. I hope you will enjoy the recipes from these wonderful homes in your very own Home of Good Food.

Hilton Park

CLONES, CO. MONAGHAN

*C*ounty Monaghan has one of the most attractive landscapes in Ireland. Although only ninety miles from Dublin, it is unspoilt by tourism, industry and urban development. The retreating glaciers from the last ice age left well-wooded gravel hills rising from a thousand lakes. In the distance lie the mountains of Fermanagh. The area has always been fertile and prosperous - John Wesley wrote in 1775 that Clones had a larger market place than any he had seen in England. In the 1730s one Samuel Madden sent his son to Clones to build a mansion close to the banks of the River Finn. His was a distinguished family of lawyers, clerics and soldiers who had come to Ireland around 1600. His house, which became known as Hilton Park, was rebuilt in 1804 and enlarged and ennobled in 1872. It is now a microcosm of a quarter of a millennium of Irish social history.

Samuel "Premium" Madden was a remarkable man - a name that Ireland ought to honour, wrote Dr. Johnson. He set up prizes for learning, arts and industry, was responsible for the Dublin Society's royal charter and wrote "A Memoir of The Twentieth Century" - in 1735. John Madden, who enlarged the house, was a noted Home Ruler and a supporter of Isaac

Butt. The present hosts of Hilton, Johnny and Lucy, are the eighth generation of Maddens to live there and they have turned the house into one of the most enchanting places to stay in the country.

Lucy is a brilliant cook. In the big old-fashioned kitchen, whose dressers are stacked with Victorian jelly moulds and antique choppers with fruitwood handles, her Aga cooker and massive pine table are as a palette and canvas to an artist. The cooking is inspired, and the lands of Hilton and the surrounding countryside produce a cornucopia of fresh organic ingredients of incomparable flavour - the Hilton organic gardens provide old-fashioned apples and vegetables to restaurants as far away as Belfast. Johnny is a most engaging host and runs the house with a quiet efficiency that demonstrates his early training under the family's butler. In every room of the house are shelves of books and the walls are decorated with a myriad ancestors. Dark mahogany glows with a patina from years of elbow grease and in the vaulted dining room, candlelight gives a romantic air to the Lucullan feasts. Upstairs half-tester beds have pure linen sheets and piles of feather pillows, as soft as swan's down. With its woodland walks and lakes, its golf course and its immense charm, Hilton Park is a treasure you'll want to keep to yourself.

A word from the chef

When choosing menus, I believe balance is very important. I like serving food that is fresh, healthy, visually pleasing, but which also has an element of self-indulgence.

Food should reflect the seasons as well. We have a large range of fruits available to us from our farm and organic garden and I often make cheeses using a variety of herbs. We also like offering some of the very good food produced locally: smoked duck breast, quail eggs and oyster mushrooms.

All cooks must be allowed their extravagances; mine are oils and I like to have a good stock of these. I'm afraid short cuts in cooking are often to the detriment of the final result, so I try to spend a good deal of time preparing meat and vegetable stocks and jams, syrups and jellies (food of the hedgerows, crab apples, rowan and elderberry) that can be the basis of so many good sauces.

Every meal should provide a balance and contrast of flavours, colours and textures that make a harmonious whole.

Lucy Madden

Lucy Madden

MENU 1
*Smoked Duck Breast with Mango and Melon
and Quail Eggs with Herb Salad
Guinea Fowl Breasts with Oyster Mushrooms and Shallots
Leek and Potato Cakes
Ring of Grapes in Wine Jelly*

MENU 2
*Warm Salad of Trout and Salmon with Pine Nuts
Walnut Bread
Herb Stuffed Loin of Pork
White Chocolate Icecream with Poached Kumquats and Star Fruit*

MENU 3
*Smoked Fish Soup with Lovage and Marigolds
Chicken and Potato Stovies
Compote of Red, White and Black Currants
with Warm Apricot Shortbread*

menu 1

SMOKED DUCK BREAST

with mango and melon & quail eggs with herb salad

SERVES 4

4 oz sliced smoked duck breasts (110 g)
1 mango or 4 fresh figs
½ honeydew melon
2 dozen quail eggs
sprigs of fresh herbs

SALAD

A handful of lambs lettuce
parsley
lovage and rocket (if available)
1 tbsp chopped mixed herbs
a dsp chopped chives to garnish

DRESSING

3 tbsp hazelnut oil
1 dsp lemon juice
salt and pepper

Cut the melon in half and remove the seeds. Using a melon baller, scoop out the melon flesh into balls, or simply cut into even sized cubes.

Skin the mango and remove the flesh from the stone and cut into cubes.

Arrange the duck slices in a fan on a serving plate.

Pile the mango and melon into the middle.

Decorate with sprigs of fresh herbs.

Place the quail eggs in cold water, bring to the boil and boil for one minute.

Plunge into cold water and peel.

Combine the ingredients for the hazelnut dressing and mix into the lambs lettuce, parsley, lovage, rocket and herbs.

Place the salad on a serving dish. Put the quail eggs on top and sprinkle with chopped chives.

GUINEA FOWL BREASTS
with oyster mushrooms and shallots

SERVES 4-6

2 guinea fowl
4 oz oyster mushrooms (110 g)
2 chopped shallots
5 fl oz chicken stock (150 ml)
2 oz butter (50 g)
sea salt and black pepper
1 dsp chopped chervil
a knob of butter

Guinea fowl is rich, so one bird will feed two people.
Cut off the breasts and sprinkle with a little sea salt and pepper.
Melt a little butter in a pan and cook the guinea breasts a few
minutes on each side.
Remove from the pan and keep warm.
Add the chopped shallots and the oyster mushrooms to the pan
(adding a little more butter if required), and cook for a few minutes
(the vegetables should be *al dente*).
Season and put on a warmed plate, laying the guinea breasts on top.
Deglaze the pan with the chicken stock and pour over the guinea
fowl.
TO SERVE: Sprinkle with chervil before serving.

LEEK AND POTATO CAKES
SERVES 4

4 leeks
8 medium potatoes
2 oz butter (50 g)
sea salt and freshly ground black pepper

Wash and cut the leeks into ½ inch lengths and soften in butter
until just tender. Put aside.
Peel and grate the potatoes, washing the grated potato well to
remove the starch. Squeeze dry in a clean cloth.
Season with sea salt and freshly ground black pepper.
Melt some butter in a frying pan and put in a little round pancake
of potato. Push down and then put on a layer of leeks.
Finish with another round of grated potato to make a sandwich of
the potatoes and the leeks.
Fry on both sides until golden and serve with the guinea fowl.

RING OF GRAPES IN WINE JELLY
SERVES 4-6

16 oz castor sugar (450 g)
16 fl oz dry white wine (450 ml)
16 fl oz water (450 ml)
1 sliced star fruit
6 kumquats
sweet cicely, sweet geranium or mint leaves (optional)
1 sachet of gelatine (4 level tsp of powdered gelatine)
juice of 1 lemon
½ lb green grapes (225 g)
1 lb black grapes (450 g)

Make a syrup with the castor sugar, wine and water. Add the sliced
star fruit, the kumquats cut in half lengthways, and add a few
leaves of sweet cicely if you have it in your garden (optional). Other
fruit such as gooseberries and elderflower can be used in season.
When the fruit is cooked remove it, and if necessary reduce the
liquid to a pint.
Put a sachet of gelatine into 2 fl oz (55 ml) of hot water and when
softened stir it well and add to the hot liquid.
At this stage you may add the lemon juice to taste.
Pour half into a 2 pint ring mould and allow to become jelly in a
freezer (this will take 10 -15 minutes).
Onto the jelly put a layer of green grapes that have been deseeded
and cut in half.
Pour over the rest of the liquid and allow to set in a fridge.
Turn it out and fill the centre with black grapes, deseeded and cut
in half.

menu 2
WARM SALAD OF TROUT & SALMON
with pine nuts

SERVES 4

4-6 oz fish per person (110 g - 175 g)
1 tbsp lemon juice
1 dsp chopped fennel or dill
mix of salad leaves - 1 lolo rosso, 6 leaves of red lettuce
1 oz pine nuts (25 g)
1 fl oz hazelnut oil (30 ml)
Sprigs of herbs for decoration e.g. fennel, dill

4 fl oz hazelnut oil (100 ml)
juice of ½ lemon
sea salt and freshly ground black pepper

Each person will need about 4-6 oz (110 g - 175 g) of fish cut into small pieces about the size of a walnut.

Season with a little lemon juice and black pepper and, if you have it, a little chopped fennel or dill.

Mix together the ingredients for the dressing.

The dressing should have a good sharp taste as this is a rich dish.

Heat the hazelnut oil in a frying pan and very quickly cook the fish pieces.

Toss the salad in the dressing.

TO SERVE: Arrange the salad leaves on individual serving plates.

Pile some fish pieces on top and sprinkle with a few pine nuts and fresh herbs.

Serve immediately.

WALNUT BREAD

¾ lb wholemeal flour (350 g)
¼ lb plain flour (110 g)
1 tbsp sesame seeds
1 tbsp sunflower seeds
1 tbsp pinhead oatmeal
1 tbsp rolled oats
1 tbsp rye flakes
1 tsp bread soda
1 tsp salt
1 oz margarine (25 g)
2 oz walnuts (50 g)
¾ pint buttermilk (425 ml)

Preheat the oven to 180°C, 350°F, Gas 4.

Mix together all the dry ingredients except the walnuts.

Rub in 1 oz of margarine.

Add the walnuts, broken into small pieces.

Stir in the buttermilk.

Put in a 2lb loaf tin.

Place in a hot oven for about 40 minutes until the bread sounds hollow when tapped on the underside.

HERB STUFFED LOIN OF PORK

SERVES 4

2 lb boned and rolled pork loin (900 g)
2 tbsp chopped fresh herbs, parsley, fennel, dill, lovage, chervil
1 full wine glass red wine
1 sprig rosemary
oil
1 small peeled onion
2 dsp redcurrant or elderberry jelly
8 fl oz veal or chicken stock (225 ml)

Preheat the oven to 200°C, 400°F, Gas 6.

Have your butcher bone and roll the pork loin.

With an apple corer make a hole through the meat and stuff this with any chopped fresh herbs you may have.

Marinade for about 4 hours in the red wine.

Drain off the marinade and keep aside.

Put a sprig of rosemary on the meat and dribble with a little oil.

Put the onion in with the meat.

Place in the oven (a 2lb/900 g piece of meat will take about 30 minutes).

Halfway through the cooking time pour off any excess fat.

Add the marinade and put a spoonful of redcurrant or elderberry jelly on top of the meat.

Lower the temperature to 180°C, 350°F, Gas 4.

When the meat is cooked, remove and keep warm.

Add a little stock to the pan, together with a spoonful of jelly and a little more wine to taste.

This goes well with Florence fennel and a green salad.

WHITE CHOCOLATE ICECREAM
with poached kumquats and star fruit

SERVES 4

5 oz white chocolate (150 g)
½ pint milk (275 ml)
3 oz castor sugar (75 g)
14 fl oz cream (400 ml)

Place the white chocolate in a double saucepan with 3 tbsp milk set over hot water.
Do not allow the water to boil.
Allow the chocolate to melt.
Dissolve the castor sugar with the rest of the milk over a gentle heat.
When it is room temperature, stir into the melted chocolate.
Whip the cream until it just holds its shape and fold it into the chocolate mixture.
Freeze in an icecream maker.
TO SERVE: Serve with poached fruit e.g. kumquats or starfruit.

menu 3

SMOKED FISH SOUP
with lovage and marigolds

SERVES 4

½ oz butter (10 g)
2 medium onions, chopped
½ lb smoked fish, haddock or cod (225 g)
½ head Florence fennel
½ lb potatoes, cubed (225 g)
1 ½ pints of milk (825 ml)
8 fl oz cream (225 ml)
a little bunch (8-10 leaves) of fresh lovage
salt and pepper
1 bayleaf
marigold petals (optional)

Melt the butter and add the chopped onions, potatoes and the fish cut into strips.
Cook until transparent.
Season, add the bay leaf and cover with milk. Bring to the boil, and simmer very gently until the potatoes are cooked.
Add the chopped lovage leaves and cream.
Heat and serve, but take care not to boil the soup at this stage.
Before serving sprinkle with marigold petals.

CHICKEN AND POTATO STOVIES
SERVES 4

1 large free-range chicken
2 lbs potatoes (900 g)
4 oz butter (110 g)
2 fat leeks
1 onion
2 tbsp dry white wine
½ pint chicken stock (275 ml)
sea salt and freshly ground black pepper

Cut the chicken up into pieces. Peel the potatoes and slice thickly.
Clean the leeks and slice.
In a wide thick saucepan, heat the butter and sauté the chicken
until lightly browned.
Add the potatoes and leeks, cover with the wine, stock and
seasonings.
Put the lid on the pan. Cook very gently for about ¾ hour until the
chicken and the potatoes are cooked.
TO SERVE: Serve with green salad.

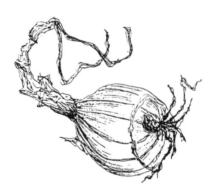

NOTE: "Stovies" comes from the French word "étouffer" meaning to stew in an enclosed
vessel.

COMPOTE of RED, WHITE and BLACK
CURRANTS *with warm apricot shortbread*

SERVES 4

1 ½ lbs fruit (fruit from the freezer can be used but
it will not have the same intensity of taste) (700 g)
3-4 oz sugar, according to taste (75 -110 g)
¾ pint water (425 ml)
1 dsp lemon juice
a few leaves of mint

Bring the sugar and water slowly to the boil, stirring to dissolve the
sugar.
Allow to boil for a few minutes and then very carefully put in the
washed and dried fruit.
Let the fruits barely simmer until they soften but do not burst.
Add lemon juice to taste and serve warm with a scattering of mint
leaves.
TO SERVE: Serve with warm apricot shortbread.

WARM APRICOT SHORTBREAD

4 oz soft brown sugar (110 g)
7 oz self raising flour (200 g)
6 oz butter (175 g)
apricot jam (preferably homemade)

Preheat oven to 180°C, 350°F, Gas 4.
Work together the brown sugar, flour and butter (this can be done
in a food processor).
Divide in two parts and press to size (cook in 2 x 7 inch sandwich
tins lined with greaseproof paper).
Bake in the oven for about 20 minutes or until nut brown.
Sandwich with very good quality (preferably homemade) apricot
jam.
Serve hot with compote of red, white and black currants. It will
keep several days in a tin and become soft when reheated.

Rathsallagh

DUNLAVIN, CO WICKLOW

*O*n the borders of Wicklow and Kildare, where the granite mountains slope down to the limestone plain of the Curragh and the young Liffey babbles between leafy banks, stands the village of Dunlavin. Following the example of the great third-century king Cormac Mac Art, who lies buried nearby beneath a brace of pillar stones, it was to Rathsallagh House at Dunlavin that Joe and Kay O'Flynn came, deserting their native Cork, in the 1970s. Even then their reputation for hospitality was famous. Cormac's philosophical treatise which describes the ideal lifestyle of his times could nearly define life at Rathsallagh nowadays. High marks for success, tipple, intelligent conversation and poetry.

In 1987 the O'Flynns opened their doors and their dining room to the public and rapidly became one of Leinster's favourite hostelries. A long avenue winds impressively through 500 acres of verdant wooded parkland

and a private golf course. Limes and Beeches, Scots Pine and Monkey Puzzle prepare one for a noble mansion. Then appearing suddenly is a long, low, ivy-clad house set around a courtyard. Where are the pillared porticoes or battlemented turrets? All gone, for in the great rising of 1798 the house burned to the ground and instead of trying to restore it the family actually did what many an Irishman longs to do - they moved into the stables.

Rather than formal grandeur, Rathsallagh is the essence of homely comfort - if you come from a very stylish home. One wing of the house is the indoor swimming pool. On the other side it is balanced by the splendid dining room where gourmets and gourmands vie with each other to consume course after course as it appears from the big farmhouse kitchen at the back of the house. And between the two wings are the drawing rooms, bedrooms and billiard room where one can relax between bouts of self-indulgence. With organic growers just down the road at Castleruddery and its own magical walled garden full of herbs and vegetables (not to mention acres of wild garlic and sorrel), local deer, sheep grazing the pastures around the house and wild duck and pheasant everywhere, this is the place to enjoy "real food".

A word from the chef

One of the most important things to remember when cooking is to use the freshest ingredients available. I am very conscious of this and tend to let the ingredients speak for themselves. Choose the best products available first. Then pick a recipe. Not the other way round.

You will notice that none of my recipes is very difficult and they are ideal for entertaining at home. No recipe should be followed to the letter of the law except the basic sauce for the cheese soufflé. Use your imagination and be inventive. Don't be afraid to try something new... for instance, the nettle and sorrel soup. This may sound unusual, but it's absolutely delicious and is full of iron. Be sure to pick young nettle leaves in a clean area (i.e. not in a spot frequented by the dog!). Nettles have the advantage of being absolutely free, and if you don't have any sorrel, you can use watercress as a substitute.

If you have your own garden, pick the salad leaves and herbs just before you need them. And if you don't have a garden, you might consider growing herbs in a window box.

Whatever you do, trust your own taste, enjoy cooking and try to make each recipe your own. If you enjoy food and can read ... you can cook.

Kay O'Flynn

Kay O'Flynn

MENU 1
Woodland Salad
Twice Baked Cheese Soufflé
Roast Rib of Beef with Fresh Horseradish and Béarnaise Sauces
Almond Baskets with Vanilla Icecream and Fresh Fruit Sauce

MENU 2
Prawns with Red Peppers
Nettle and Sorrel Soup
Baked Spiced Bacon with Garlic Potatoes
Crème Brûlée

MENU 3
Peach and Tomato Soup
Mussels Rathsallagh
Roast Pheasant with Game Chips and Buttered Crumbs
Malva Pudding

menu 1

WOODLAND SALAD

SERVES 4

1 crisp butterhead lettuce
a handful of lambs lettuce
a few leaves of rocket (optional)
wild garlic leaves and flowers (optional, may substitute
nasturtiums, borage, violas or salad burnet)
8 quail eggs (boiled for 3 minutes)
about 8 wild mushrooms or oyster mushrooms lightly cooked in a
little good olive oil
1 slice of bread cut into croutons and fried until golden brown
2 lardons of bacon fried till crisp
a bunch of chives

DRESSING

1 tbsp of champagne vinegar (or white wine vinegar)
2 tbsp olive oil
1 tbsp of hazelnut oil
salt and pepper
1 garlic clove, crushed
pinch of Dijon mustard

Thoroughly wash all the salad leaves.
Arrange the leaves on a plate with the eggs, croutons, lardons and
mushrooms.
Mix the dressings together very well.
Sprinkle the dressing lightly over the salad plate just before serving.
Arrange long strands of chives on top with garlic flowers.
Alternatively this dish can be served on 4 salad plates for
individual servings.
TO SERVE: Serve with crusty brown bread.

TWICE BAKED CHEESE SOUFFLÉ
SERVES 4

½ pint of milk (275 ml)
slice of onion
pinch of grated nutmeg
knob of butter
2 oz butter (50 g)
2 oz plain flour (50 g)
pinch of dry mustard
6 oz mixed grated cheese i.e. Cashel Blue, Red Cheddar (175 g)
4 eggs and 1 egg white
salt and pepper
12 fl oz cream (330 ml)

Heat the oven to 180°C, 350°F, Gas 4.

Heat the milk gently with the onion and nutmeg.

Melt the knob of butter and grease 4 straight-sided teacups or individual soufflé dishes.

Separate the eggs.

Melt the remaining butter and stir in the flour and mustard. Cook for a moment.

Remove from the heat and add the milk and ¾ of the cheese.

Add the egg yolks to the cheese sauce.

Season.

Whip the egg whites until stiff. Fold into the sauce gently.

Spoon into cups until ⅔ full.

Stand in a bain marie and bake for 15 minutes or until risen and set.

Allow to sink and cool.

Turn out on to a plate until ready to serve.

TO SERVE: Place the soufflés upside down on a big dish or individual dishes.

Set the oven to 220°C, 425°F or Gas 7.

Sprinkle with the remaining cheese.

Pour the cream over.

Bake for 15 minutes until a pale gold.

Serve immediately.

NOTE: Bain marie: A roasting tin half filled with hot water, in which terrines etc are cooked. This is to protect the food from direct heat.

ROAST RIB OF BEEF
with fresh horseradish and béarnaise sauces

SERVES 6-8

*3 ribs of beef
some beef dripping
fresh ground black pepper
salt*

Set the oven to 200°C, 400°F, Gas 6. Have the beef at room temperature.
Season with pepper only.
Heat the dripping in a roasting tin.
Baste the beef and roast for 1 hour for rare, 1 hour 20 minutes for medium and 1 ½ hours for well done.
Approximately 10 minutes before the end of the cooking time sprinkle the fat side only with coarse sea salt.
Rest for at least 10 minutes before carving.

HORSERADISH SAUCE

*¼ pint cream (150 ml)
1 ½ - 2 tbsp fresh grated horseradish
2 tsp wine vinegar
½ tsp dry mustard
salt and white pepper
pinch of cayenne pepper
squeeze of lemon juice*

Whip the cream very lightly and fold in the remaining ingredients.

BÉARNAISE SAUCE

*2 tbsp wine vinegar
6 black peppercorns
1 bay leaf
1 small onion, chopped
sprig fresh tarragon
sprig of parsley
2 egg yolks
4 oz butter (110 g)
1 tsp fresh tarragon, chopped
1 tsp parsley, chopped*

Reduce the vinegar with the bay leaf, onion and sprigs of herbs and peppercorns to 1 tbsp.

Strain the vinegar and return to the pot. Add the butter and melt to foaming point.

Whip the egg yolks with a pinch of salt in a food processor. With the machine still running, pour in the butter in a steady stream. Whip for a few seconds. Pour into a clean lukewarm thermos until ready to serve.

ALMOND BASKETS
with vanilla icecream and fresh fruit sauce

SERVES 4

ALMOND BASKETS
1 oz blanched almonds (25 g)
2 egg whites
4 oz castor sugar (110 g)
2 oz plain flour (50 g)
drop of vanilla essence
2 oz melted butter (50 g)

Preheat the oven to 180°C , 350°F, Gas 4.

Grease 3 baking sheets.

Shred the almonds.

Beat the sugar into the egg whites with a fork. Stir in the flour and add the vanilla and almonds. Mix with a fork.

Ensure the melted butter has cooled. Add to the mixture and stir.

Place teaspoons of the mixture 5 inches apart and flatten on baking sheets. Only do a few at a time.

Bake for 5-6 minutes until brown at the edges and pale in the middle.

Cool for a few seconds.

Lift carefully and place one at a time on a greased upturned tumbler or tartlet tin.

Cool and store in an airtight container until needed.

VANILLA ICECREAM
4 eggs, separated
2 x ½ pint cartons of cream (570 ml)
4 oz icing sugar (110 g)
drop of vanilla essence

Whisk the egg whites until stiff.

Gradually add in the sugar, whisking until stiff.

Beat the egg yolks lightly.

Whisk the cream until it holds a light trail.

Fold everything together and freeze.

FRUIT SAUCE

In a blender or food processor liquidise a mix of about 1lb (450 g) of assorted fruits (strawberries, raspberries, red currants and blackcurrants). Sieve.

Add sugar to taste.

Add some stewed rhubarb if desired.

TO SERVE: Pour some sauce on each plate.

Place an almond basket in the centre and fill with icecream.

Garnish with fresh fruit.

menu 2
PRAWNS WITH RED PEPPERS

SERVES 4

1 lb Dublin Bay prawns, cooked and shelled (450 g)
1 medium sized red pepper, sliced and seeded
1 small red onion, thinly sliced
1 small lemon, thinly sliced
1 stick celery, sliced
2 ½ fl oz sunflower oil (70 ml)
2 ½ fl oz olive oil (70 ml)
1 tsp dry mustard
2 fl oz champagne vinegar (or white wine vinegar) (55 ml)
½ oz stoned black olives (10 g)
juice of 2 lemons
dash of Worcester Sauce
dash of Tabasco
salt and pepper
1 tsp sugar

Whisk oils, vinegar, lemon juice, sauces, seasonings, mustards and sugar together.

Place everything else in a pottery or china dish.

Pour the dressing over.

Cover and chill for 24 hours.

TO SERVE: Serve with crusty French bread, brushed with olive oil and garlic and toasted under the grill.

NETTLE AND SORREL SOUP
SERVES 4

1 onion, chopped
2 oz butter (50 g)
3 leeks, chopped
1 stick celery, chopped
1 clove of garlic, crushed
big bunch of nettles (use rubber gloves to handle
and be careful where you pick them)
1 small bunch of sorrel
3 medium potatoes
salt and freshly ground black pepper
parsley, thyme, bay leaf and fresh oregano
1 ½ pints of chicken stock (850 ml)
½ pint creamy milk (275 ml)

Sweat the onions, leeks, carrots and celery in the butter until soft.
Add the garlic and chopped potato, herbs, seasonings and chicken
stock. Bring to the boil.
Simmer until the vegetables are cooked, about 15 minutes.
Add the nettles and sorrel and cook for another 5 minutes.
Liquidise and sieve back into a clean saucepan.
Add the milk, check seasoning, reheat and serve.

BAKED SPICED BACON
with garlic potatoes

SERVES 4-6

2 ½ - 3 lbs loin of green bacon
(not too salty, ask your butcher to check) (1 kg 150 g - 1 kg 350 g)
4 large cloves of garlic, finely chopped
1 large onion, roughly chopped
4 tsp ground cumin
1 lb tomatoes, chopped (450 g)
2 bay leaves
2 sprigs of thyme
1 tbsp chopped oregano
3 tbsp good quality olive oil
2 dsp white wine vinegar
2 lbs potatoes, peeled and cut in large chunks (900 g)
black pepper
4 tbsp chopped parsley

Soak the bacon in cold water in a cool place for 24 hours. Change the water a number of times.

Take the bacon out of the water and dry it thoroughly in a clean cloth.

Mix ⅓ garlic with ½ cumin and plenty of freshly ground black pepper. Rub all over the meat and leave to stand in the fridge for at least 3-4 hours.

Mix together the potatoes with the onion, tomatoes, cumin and remaining garlic and black pepper. Lay the mixture in the bottom of an oven-proof, thick casserole.

Pour over the oil and vinegar and add the herbs. Mix it all up and place the bacon on top of the potatoes, and cover lightly.

Cook in a preheated oven 180°C, 350°F, Gas 4 for 2 - 2 ½ hours. Take out the bacon and peel the skin.

TO SERVE: Put a spoon of potato mixture onto a plate, dust with parsley and place thin slices of bacon on top. Serve the extra potatoes separately, thickly dusted with chopped parsley.

CRÈME BRÛLÉE
SERVES 4

1 pint cream (570 ml)
4 egg yolks
2 tbsp sugar
1 vanilla pod

Preheat the oven to 150°C, 300°F, Gas 2.

In a double saucepan bring the cream with the vanilla pod to just under boiling point.

Remove the pod.

Cream the egg yolks and 1 tablespoon of sugar together with a wooden spoon.

Slowly add the cream, stirring all the time.

Pour back into the double saucepan and stir over the heat until the mixture coats the back of a wooden spoon.

Strain into a shallow oven-proof dish.

Place in a heated oven for about 3-5 minutes until a skin forms on top.

Remove and cool.

Place in a fridge until chilled.

Preheat the grill to high.

Sprinkle the remaining sugar on top and grill for a few minutes until the sugar caramelises.

Chill and serve with red currants.

menu 3

PEACH AND TOMATO SOUP

SERVES 4

2 large onions, chopped
2 carrots, chopped
3 potatoes, chopped
small head celery, chopped
2 cloves garlic, chopped
2 15oz tins of tomatoes (850 g)
2 fresh peaches, chopped
1 tbsp icing sugar
salt and freshly ground black pepper
2 pints chicken stock (1l 140ml)
1 oz butter (25 g)
1 bay leaf
1 sprig of thyme

Sweat the onion, carrot and celery in butter.

Add the potato, garlic, tomatoes and chicken stock.

Simmer for 20 minutes until the vegetables are cooked.

Liquidise and sieve.

Liquidise the peaches with the sugar and add to the soup.

Check seasonings.

Add more stock if the soup is too thick.

* Do not add peaches until the day of serving.

If you wish to freeze the soup, defrost and then add the peaches.

Ring of Grapes in Wine Jelly, see page 15

Guinea Fowl Breasts with Oyster Mushrooms, see page 14

Smoked Duck Breast, Quail Eggs and Herb Salad, see page 13

The Music Room at Hilton Park

Almond Baskets with Vanilla Icecream, see page 28

Roast Rib of Beef, see page 27

Twice Baked Cheese Soufflé, see page 26

Drawing Room Fireplace at Rathsallagh

Pheasant and Pigeon Terrine with Blackcurrant Sauce, see page 47

Irish Mist Soufflé, see page 50

A Bedroom at Marlfield House

Entrance Foyer at Marlfield

MUSSELS RATHSALLAGH
SERVES 4

3 lbs mussels (1 kg 350g)
1 glass white wine
approx. 6fl oz (175 ml) water
1 small shallot, chopped
2 cloves garlic
1 tbsp chopped parsley
black pepper
julienne of carrot, onion and celery, about 2 tbsps
½ pint measure of rice (275 ml)
1 pint water (570 ml)
2 oz butter (50 g)
1 tbsp cream

Scrub the mussels well and check to see that they are tightly closed.
Leave for a few hours in a cold place in plenty of fresh water and a
fistful of porridge oats.
Rinse well again.
Put the 6 fl oz of water in a frying pan and bring to the boil. Add
the mussels in single layers, and cook gently until they open (2-3
minutes). Remove them from the pan when they open.
Discard any that do not open.
Remove one shell as soon as they are cool enough to handle.
Reserve the liquid.
Blanch the vegetables and refresh under cold running water.
Meanwhile cook the rice in a covered saucepan over a gentle heat
in one pint of boiling salted water, until all the water is absorbed.
Strain the liquid from the mussels through muslin into a clean
saucepan.
Add the wine, garlic and pepper.
Boil for 1-2 minutes.
Add the vegetables and mussels.
Reheat gently.
Toss the rice in melted butter. Add the cream and parsley to the
sauce.
TO SERVE: Divide the rice between 4-6 plates. Ladle the mussels and
sauce over the rice and serve with a wedge of lemon.

ROAST PHEASANT
with game chips and buttered crumbs

SERVES 2

1 plump pheasant, plucked and cleaned
6 juniper berries, crushed
1 small chopped cooking apple
1 small onion, chopped
4 oz butter (110 g)
salt and black pepper
juice of 1 small orange
3 oz butter (75 g)
½ pint game stock (275 ml)
1 tbsp Calvados

Preheat the oven to 190°C, 375°F, Gas 5.

Make sure the pheasant is clean and dry.

Cook the onions and apple gently in the orange juice and a knob of butter until softened.

Add the juniper berries, salt and pepper.

Stuff the cavity of the bird with the mixture.

Melt the remaining butter and rub all over the pheasant. Season.

Place the pheasant on one breast side, baste and roast for 15 minutes.

Turn onto the other side, baste and roast for 15 minutes.

Turn onto its back and cook again for 15 minutes.

Check the legs to see if the bird is cooked.

Remove from the pan.

Deglaze the pan with the stock and add the Calvados.

Cook, stirring up all the sediment and juice.

Strain and serve in a sauce-boat.

Serve with fresh breadcrumbs cooked slowly until brown and crisp in butter, and game chips. (A packet of crisps can be substituted for the game chips)

GAME CHIPS

4 medium potatoes
oil for frying

Peel the potatoes and slice very finely.

Soak in cold water to remove the starch; dry thoroughly.

Heat cooking oil in a large frying pan. Sprinkle the potato slices on top, taking care that they do not stick to each other.

When golden brown, remove, drain and sprinkle with salt.

MALVA PUDDING
SERVES 4

6 oz sugar (175 g)
1 egg
1 tbsp apricot jam
6 oz flour (175 g)
1 tsp bread soda
a pinch of salt
1 oz butter (25 g)
1 tsp vinegar
1 teacup of milk

SAUCE

1 teacup of cream
6 oz butter (175 g)
6 oz sugar (175 g)
½ cup hot water

Preheat the oven to 180°C, 350°F, Gas 4.
Beat the eggs, sugar and jam together.
Sieve the flour, bread soda and salt.
Melt the butter and add the vinegar.
Begin adding the milk and flour to the egg mixture, alternating the milk and flour.
When all the milk mixture and seasoned flour has been incorporated, add the vinegar and butter and mix well.
Pour into an ovenproof dish and cover with tinfoil.
Bake for ¾ hour.
The pudding is cooked when it is a rich brown colour all over.
Melt together the ingredients for the sauce.
Pour over the pudding as it comes out of the oven.
If you reheat it and it is slightly dry, pour a little boiling water over the pudding.
Serve with whipped cream.

Marlfield

GOREY, CO WEXFORD

*I*n the beginning there was in Curracloe a house with a pretty garden
where Mary Bowe and her family lived and ran a small restaurant.
*Esker Lodge, as the house was called, was an oasis of good food in the
culinary desert that was Ireland in the 1970s. On a well deserved weekend
break at Longueville, basking in the sybaritic luxury of breakfast in bed,
Mary turned to her husband, Ray, and said, "We should have a country
house like this." A lady of action, she had bought Marlfield House in Gorey
within a week. What was the modest dower house of the Earls of Courtown
is now most remarkable. Between the hinterland of Gorey and the seaside
charms of Courtown, the post-modernist steel entrance gates with their
skeletal pineapples are a surprise. The Victorian conservatory, with its
tropical murals and cast iron trellis from Brighton railway station, is
astonishing; and the suites, larger than an average townhouse, with beds
the size of swimming pools hidden discreetly behind sliding walls and an
eighteenth-century print room decoration executed by Marina Guinness,*

are amazing. The hotel is furnished with a highly decorative collection of antiques - Mary Bowe must have a memento from every country house sale in Ireland, right down to the linen traycloths which came from Christie's multi-million pound sale at Luttrelstown Castle.

During the great rising of 1798 the houses around Gorey were all burnt to the ground. The Stopford family rebuilt Courtown House around 1820 and at the same time built Marlfield, just a mile down the road, as a dower house, primarily for younger sons rather than widowed mothers (the usual role of a dower house). In 1947 the Irish Tourist Board compulsorily acquired Courtown House to turn it into a showpiece hotel. They then decided it was in need of too much restoration and so demolished it. The family in the meantime had moved into Marlfield. Not until they sold it could private enterprise, in the shape of Mary Bowe, create on Ireland's east coast a showpiece country house hotel of style and warmth, beauty and charm - an example to all hoteliers. More elegant and sophisticated than ever it was, the heyday of Marlfield is now, rather than lying in some noble past. A convenient supper stop before the opera at Wexford, a charming luncheon place for diplomats to bring their guests from Dublin, Marlfield is a monument to Mary Bowe's single-minded dedication to excellence.

A word from the chef

Eating out, above all, should be for the enjoyment of the customer, and providing good food and service, the aim of the restaurateur. This philosophy can equally be applied to entertainment at home. There has never been a more exciting time to be a cook and to appreciate to the full all the marvellous produce that is nowadays at our disposal. The best of each season's vegetables, meat and fish should determine the chef's individual dishes and the menu as a whole. I wholeheartedly believe that the chef must spend time daily, if at all possible, examining the fresh produce on offer and buying accordingly.

Strolling around the vegetable and herb garden in Marlfield in the spring and summer, I like to see all the lovely colourful vegetables and heavenly scented flowering herbs. Their different shapes, colours and textures inspire me to create from them lovely terrines and hors d'oeuvres. I believe a constant supply of fresh herbs is essential for every good restaurant. The judicious addition of the right fresh herb will give any dish that extra special flavour which will make it worthy of the best table. Artistic arrangement and presentation of dishes is essential and sauces should be the perfectly harmonious accompaniment to the individual dishes. A supreme cook is recognised by his or her sauces.

Rose Brannock

Rose Brannock

MENU 1

Pheasant and Pigeon Terrine with Pear Purée and a Blackcurrant Sauce
Light Braised Noisettes of Pork with Roast Shallots in a Calvados Sauce
Irish Mist Soufflé with a Crème de Menthe and Chocolate Sauce
Petit Four Honey Truffles

MENU 2
*Timbale of Chicken Mousse Stuffed with Crabmeat with a Light Mustard
Seed Sauce
Orange and Mint Sorbet
Grilled Fillets of Sole and Monkfish with Fresh Asparagus and a Tomato
and Chive Sauce
Pineapple and Mango Crêpe with a Champagne Sabayon*

MENU 3
*Warm Salad of Baby Spinach with Veal Sweetbreads and Saffron
Vinaigrette
Cream of Parsley and Chive Soup
Lightly Baked Fillets of Turbot on a Bed of Warm Pink Grapefruit
Layered Cinnamon Biscuits with Pastry Cream, Fresh Cherries and a
Cherry Brandy Syrup*

menu 1

PHEASANT AND PIGEON TERRINE
with pear purée and a blackcurrant sauce

SERVES 6

TERRINE

*1 pheasant
6 pigeon breasts
zest of 1 orange
zest of 1 lemon
5 shallots
1 clove of garlic, minced
1 apple
6 slices of bacon
1 ½ fl oz egg white (45 ml)
½ oz butter (10 g)
nutmeg and seasoning
1 oz pistachio nuts (25 g), 6 inch terrine mould*

Remove the breasts and legs from the pheasant.
Remove the skin and bone, and cut the legs.
Mince the meat from the pheasant and leave to chill in the fridge.
Dice the shallots and apple finely.
Melt the butter, sauté the shallots, garlic and apple.
When soft, add the zests of orange and lemon, and leave to cool.
Place the mince into the food processor with the egg white and mix
for a minute or two.

Remove from the food processor and mix in the cold shallots, garlic, apple and citrus zests.

Season with nutmeg, salt and pepper.

Season the pigeon breasts and lightly cook in the frying pan.

Leave to cool. Lightly grease the terrine mould, and line with the bacon.

Layer the pheasant mix with the pigeon breasts.

Place into a bain marie and cook for 45 mins - 1 hour in a moderate oven 180°C, 350°F, Gas 4.

PEAR PURÉE

2 pears
1 oz sugar (25 g)
3 fl oz water (75 ml)

Boil the sugar and water. Peel and core the pears.

Cook in the stock syrup. When soft, liquidise.

Leave to cool.

BLACKCURRANT SAUCE

¼ lb blackcurrants (110 g)
1 oz sugar (25 g)
3 fl oz water (75 ml)
2 teaspoons crème de cassis

Remove the stalks from the blackcurrants.

Cook with the sugar and water.

Add the crème de cassis in at the end.

When the blackcurrants are soft, liquidise and pass through a fine strainer.

TO SERVE: Serve cold, cut into slices, with some of the pear purée and blackcurrant sauce.

LIGHTLY BRAISED NOISETTES OF PORK
with roast shallots in a Calvados sauce

SERVES 4

2 pork fillets
20 shallots
sage and parsley
salt and freshly ground pepper
oil

CALVADOS SAUCE

2 ½ fl oz Calvados (70 ml)
1 pt demi-glaze (570 ml)
10 diced shallots
2 oz button mushrooms (50 g)

Place a large deep pan on the stove. When hot add a little oil and sweat the diced shallots and mushrooms.
Add the Calvados and leave to cook for a minute or two.
Add the demi-glaze and leave to cook until it starts to reduce.
Pass through a fine strainer. Peel the remaining shallots.
Trim the pork fillets, removing all fat and excess meat.
Cut into noisettes, season and sprinkle with sage and parsley.
Lightly brown in a hot pan, then remove and leave to one side.
Lightly colour the shallots in a frying pan for a few minutes; remove from the oven and leave with the pork fillet. Add the pork noisettes and shallots to the sauce and leave to cook for a few minutes.

DEMI-GLAZE

3 tbsp oil
2 small carrots
1 small onion
1 stick celery
1 tbsp flour
1 pint brown stock
½ tsp tomato purée
a few mushroom peelings
bouquet garni

Cut the vegetables into fine dice.
Heat the oil and cook the vegetables till brown. Stir in the flour and cook slowly till brown.

Take off the heat, add ¾ pint of stock and the remaining ingredients.
Bring to the boil and simmer for 30 minutes, removing any scum that comes to the surface.
Strain and season.

IRISH MIST SOUFFLÉ
with a crème de menthe and chocolate sauce

SERVES 8

3 oz sugar (50 g)
3 egg yolks
3 egg whites
½ pt cream (275 ml)
2 ½ leaves of gelatine (2 ¼ heaped tsp powdered gelatine)
2 fl oz Irish Mist (55 ml)

Soak the gelatine in water until soft.
Beat the yolks and sugar together until white.
Lightly whip the cream. Lightly whip the egg whites.
Dissolve the gelatine in the Irish Mist and add to the egg and sugar mix.
Mix in the cream and fold in the egg whites.
Place in dariole moulds and leave in the fridge to set.

CRÈME DE MENTHE & CHOCOLATE SAUCE

3 egg yolks
1 oz sugar
½ pt milk
2 tsp of crème de menthe
1 oz chocolate melted

Boil the milk. Beat the egg yolks and sugar together until white.
Add in the milk and whisk.
Put back on the stove and cook over a slow heat, stirring constantly until it coats the back of the spoon. Halve the mixture.
When cool add in the crème de menthe to one half. Taste.
Using the other half of warm vanilla sauce, add in the melted chocolate and mix together thoroughly.
Turn the dariole mould onto a plate, place the crème de menthe on one half of the plate and the chocolate sauce on the other.

NOTE: Turn out just before serving. This will only turn out from individual dariole moulds; otherwise place in a large bowl, chill for 4 hours and serve from the bowl. If necessary put in the freezer briefly.

PETIT FOUR HONEY TRUFFLES

5 oz butter (150 g)
4 oz marzipan (110 g)
4 ½ oz honey (125 g)
7 oz white chocolate (200 g)
7 oz milk chocolate (200 g)
vanilla essence
2 tsp brandy
2 oz toasted almonds (50 g) for garnish

Have the butter and marzipan at room temperature.
Beat together until they are thoroughly mixed.
Add in the honey, vanilla essence and brandy, and mix together.
Melt both chocolates in a double saucepan.
Mix in both chocolates to the butter and marzipan. Leave to chill in
the fridge.
Finally, when almost set, pipe into petit four cases and place a
toasted almond on top.

menu 2

TIMBALE OF CHICKEN MOUSSE
stuffed with crabmeat with a light mustard seed sauce

SERVES 8

CHICKEN MOUSSE

2 chicken breasts
2 egg whites
½ pt cream (275 ml)
salt and pepper
melted butter
1 dsp mustard seeds to coat timbale
4 oz crabmeat (110 g)
lemon juice

MUSTARD SEED SAUCE

½ pt chicken stock (275 ml)
2 fl oz Noilly Prat (55 ml) (white wine may be substituted)
1 tsp Dijon mustard
4 shallots
½ pt double cream (275 ml)
salt and pepper, 1 dsp mustard seeds
8 dariole moulds

Cut the chicken into strips and mince.

Place the mince in a food processor, add the egg white and mix well. Remove from the food processor and pass the chicken mix through a sieve to remove any sinews. Leave to chill in the fridge.

When chilled, mix in the cream gradually and season to taste. Place back in the fridge.

Moisten the crabmeat with lemon juice and place in the fridge.

Lightly butter dariole moulds and sprinkle some mustard seeds around the sides and bottom.

Place the chicken mousse in a piping bag with a medium plain nozzle.

Pipe the chicken mousse around the edge of the darioles, leaving room for the crabmeat to be placed in the middle.

Place the crabmeat in the centre and cover with the chicken mousse.

Cover the darioles with buttered tin foil, place in a bain marie and cook for 10-15 minutes at 150°C, 300°F, Gas 2.

MUSTARD SEED SAUCE

Lightly cook the shallots in a little butter, add the Noilly Prat and leave to reduce for a few minutes.

Add the Dijon mustard and chicken stock, and leave to reduce.

Add in the cream and cook the sauce for a few minutes more until it starts to thicken.

When cooked pass through a fine strainer, return to the heat, season and add the mustard seeds.

Remove the darioles from the oven, turn out onto warm plates and cut a triangle out of the side allowing the crabmeat to fall out.

Place the sauce around the plate and garnish with sprigs of dill.

ORANGE AND MINT SORBET
SERVES 4

8 fl oz fresh orange juice (225 ml)
2 oz sugar (50 g)
4 fl oz water (125 ml)
2 ½ fl oz Grand Marnier
sprigs of mint

Place the sugar, water and mint sprigs in a saucepan. Bring to the boil, leave to cool and infuse the flavour of the mint.
When cold add the orange juice and Grand Marnier.
Place in a sorbetière and leave to mix for 20-25 minutes and freeze.
TO SERVE: Serve in wide champagne glasses with a sprig of mint on top.

GRILLED FILLETS OF SOLE & MONKFISH
with fresh asparagus and a tomato and chive sauce

SERVES 4

4 sole fillets
1 small monkfish tail
lemon juice
salt and freshly ground black pepper
flour, butter
8 asparagus tips

TOMATO AND CHIVE SAUCE

16 oz ripe tomatoes
½ pt fish stock (275 ml)
basil
chives
6 diced shallots
2 cloves garlic
1 tsp sugar
oil
seasoning

Wash and halve the tomatoes, dice the shallots.
Heat a saucepan, and add the oil, tomatoes and shallots; cook for a few minutes.
Add the garlic, herbs and sugar, and mix well.
Add in the fish stock and leave to cook for 10 minutes.

When cooked, liquidise and pass through a strainer; place back on the heat and season, and add in chopped chives just before serving.

SOLE AND MONKFISH

Grease a baking tray with butter, and place the sole fillets on the tray; sprinkle with lemon juice, lightly butter and season.
Sprinkle the monkfish with lemon juice, season, lightly flour and brown in a hot pan; place on the tray with the sole and cook under the grill.

ASPARAGUS

Blanch the asparagus tips in boiling water with a little lemon juice added.
Place the sole and monkfish on a warm joint plate, arrange the asparagus around it, pour the sauce onto the plate and decorate with chive flowers.

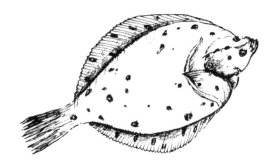

PINEAPPLE AND MANGO CRÊPE
with a champagne sabayon

SERVES 8

4 ½ oz flour (125 g)
½ oz sugar (15 g)
2 eggs
11 fl oz milk, boiled and cooled (325 ml)
3 ½ fl oz cream (100 ml)
½ oz clarified butter (15 g)

Mix the flour, sugar and salt in a bowl.
Add the eggs. Stir in one-third of the milk until the mix is smooth.
Pour in the cream and remaining milk.
Leave in a cool place to rest for at least an hour.

PINEAPPLE AND MANGO

Peel the pineapple and mango and cut into inch-size pieces.
Heat a pan, add a little clarified butter and sauté the fruit gently.
Keep warm until required.

TO COOK PANCAKES

Stir the batter.
Heat a frying pan and brush with clarified butter.
Pour in a little batter and allow to cook for 1-2 minutes on each side.
Turn with a palate knife and toss it.
TO SERVE: Roll each crêpe or fold in half with the mixture in the centre.
Pour a little prepared champagne sabayon over each crêpe and brown under the grill.
Decorate with some mint leaves and serve immediately.

CHAMPAGNE SABAYON

4 egg yolks
3 oz sugar
3 fl oz champagne

Combine the egg yolks, sugar and champagne in a shallow pan.
Place the pan over a bain marie of water and whisk until it reaches the ribbon stage. Never make the sabayon too soon in advance.

menu 3

WARM SALAD OF BABY SPINACH
with veal sweetbreads and saffron vinaigrette

SERVES 4

SAFFRON VINAIGRETTE

2 tsp French mustard
2 fl oz white wine vinegar
2 fl oz sunflower oil (150 ml)
2 fl oz peanut oil (150 ml)
2 fl oz chive oil (150 ml)
pinch of saffron (150 ml)
1 lb spinach (450 g)

Soak the saffron in white wine vinegar.
Whisk the vinegar mixture into the mustard.
Gently whisk in the remaining oils. Season.
Wash the spinach leaves and remove stalks.

VEAL SWEETBREADS

8 oz sweetbreads - cleaned and trimmed of all waste (225 g)
egg-wash (1 egg, beaten lightly)
chopped herbs

BOUILLON

1 carrot, chopped
1 small onion, chopped
parsley stalks
seasoning
bay leaf
2 pt water (1l 140 ml)

Place all the ingredients for the bouillon into a heavy-bottomed
saucepan, bring to the boil and simmer.
Place the sweetbreads in the bouillon and cook until firm.
Refresh in cold water.
Drain, and when cool slice ¼ inch thick, dip in the egg-wash and
season.
Heat a pan and add clarified butter, add the sweetbreads and cook
until golden.
Add chopped fresh herbs to finish.
TO SERVE: Place on a bed of baby spinach and dress with warm
saffron vinaigrette

NOTE: Only young spinach is nice when raw. If not available, substitute other salad leaves.

56

CREAM OF PARSLEY & CHIVE SOUP
SERVES 4

1 cup of chopped parsley
1 cup of chopped chives
2 leeks, cleaned and chopped
4 sticks celery, cleaned and chopped
1 onion, diced
4 potatoes, peeled
1 pt chicken stock (570 ml)
¼ pt cream (150 ml)
2 oz butter (50 g)
salt and pepper

Melt the butter, add the leeks, celery and onions.
Cook over a slow heat for a few minutes.
Add the diced, peeled potatoes and herbs, keeping back a small amount of chives and parsley for garnish.
Stir and cook for a few minutes.
Add in the chicken stock and leave to cook for 45 minutes.
Liquidise and pass through a strainer, bring back to the boil, add the cream and season. Add in the remaining chives and parsley.
TO SERVE: Serve in a warm bowl with a teaspoon of lightly whipped cream and a sprinkling of chopped chives and parsley.

LIGHTLY BAKED FILLETS OF TURBOT
on a bed of warm pink grapefruit with chervil scented butter

SERVES 4

8 small fillets of turbot
2 small pink grapefruits, cut into segments

CHERVIL SCENTED BUTTER

8 oz unsalted butter (225 g)
2 bunches fresh chervil
salt and pepper
lemon juice

TO MAKE BUTTER

Melt the butter. Add the chervil and leave to infuse for 15 minutes over a gentle heat.
Add the lemon juice and season.
Strain and leave on the side to keep warm.

TO COOK TURBOT

Butter a baking tray, and place the turbot on it. Sprinkle with lemon juice, coat in butter and season with salt and pepper.
Bake in the oven for 3 minutes at 180°C, 350°F, Gas 4.
Heat the grapefruit segments on a servicing plate under the grill for a few seconds. Place the turbot on top and give it a quick flash under the grill; lightly spoon the butter over the turbot and garnish with lemon zest and sprigs of chervil.

LAYERED CINNAMON BISCUITS
with pastry cream, fresh cherries and cherry brandy syrup

SERVES 4

CINNAMON BISCUITS

2 oz unsalted butter (50 g)
2 ½ oz castor sugar (60 g)
2 ½ oz flour (60 g)
2 ½ fl oz egg white (60 g)
Pinch of cinnamon

1 ½ lb cherries

Preheat the oven to 180°C, 350°F, Gas 4.
Cream the butter and sugar together.

Bring the egg whites to room temperature. Add the whites to the butter, beating well. Fold in the flour, then rest in the fridge. Grease and flour a baking tray. Spread out the paste evenly into small circular discs onto the greased tray using the back of a teaspoon.

Bake until brown and remove from the tray onto a wire rack immediately. Allow to cool.

PASTRY CREAM

½ pt milk (275 ml)
2 oz castor sugar (50 g)
3 egg yolks
1 oz flour (25 g)
vanilla essence

In a saucepan, bring the milk and vanilla essence up to the boil. Whisk the egg yolks and sugar and mix in the flour.

Pour the boiled milk onto the egg mixture.

Put in a clean saucepan and cook gently until it thickens, taking care not to boil it or it will curdle. Remove and place in a clean bowl with greased paper over until required.

TO PREPARE CHERRIES

Allow 20 cherries per person - 14 to put between the layers and 6 to put into the syrup. Wash and halve the cherries and remove stones.

CHERRY BRANDY SYRUP

4 oz cherries (110 g)
4 fl oz stock syrup (125 ml)
2 measures cherry brandy

Heat a saucepan and add the cherry brandy; add in the fresh cherries and flambée. Add in the stock syrup and leave to cook for 10-15 minutes until it reduces and becomes syrupy.

TO SERVE: Pipe a tiny rosette of pastry cream onto each plate, place a cinnamon biscuit on top. Pipe enough pastry cream to cover the biscuit. Place half of the cherries on top then cover with another cinnamon biscuit. Repeat one more layer and finish by pouring some cherry brandy syrup around the plate.

NOTE: To make stock syrup, dissolve 4 oz sugar (110 g) in 4 fl oz of water (125 ml).

Longueville

MALLOW, CO. CORK

*I*n 1543 Donough O'Callaghan built himself a castle on a cliff over the
River Blackwater at Dromaneen. A wild bunch, his family. There was
Connor garriff "the rough" and Cahir modora "the surly" and the name
Callaghan itself is derived from ceallach, "strife". Descendants of
Ceallachan Cashel, the King of Munster who drove out the Danes in 952,
they ruled much of Cork until 1649 when Oliver Cromwell outlawed them
all. Some went to Clare, some to France, some to Baden-Baden and the
present chieftain's family went to Spain where they became lawyers. A few,
however, took to the woods of the Blackwater Valley.

In the meantime their lands fell into the hands of the Longfield family
who around 1720 built an elegant residence overlooking the ruins of
Dromaneen. In 1795, when they became Barons Longueville, the house
was made even grander with an Ionic porch and long two-storey wings.

Trees were planted in the formation of the battle lines of the French and British armies at Waterloo. Then in 1938 Senator William O'Callaghan, one of the sylvan branch, bought the house back from the Longfields.

His son Michael was, and is, a farmer and when he inherited the house, sixteen bedrooms seemed slightly surplus to requirements. However the steady flow of Killarney-bound tourists passing their gates tempted him and his wife Jane to hang a shingle offering bed and breakfast. Their hospitality became famous, but food was a problem - there were no restaurants nearby. Using fresh ingredients from their 500 acre farm and fish from the Blackwater, Jane started to provide dinner for the guests. Her reputation as an excellent cook was quickly established and the restaurant has been featured in Irish food guides for most of the 25 years that it has been open.

However, recently the food has changed from being what the Michelin Guide would call "excellent cuisine, worth a detour" to "the best cuisine, worth a journey". Michael's son William has taken charge of the kitchen. He has trained under several of the top European chefs and, in particular, Raymond Blanc, but his style is uniquely his own. Like the house, which combines the grandeur of a stately mansion with the informal hospitality of a Cork farming family, William blends the sophistication of classic modern cuisine with an appreciation of more traditional country dishes. The result is a combination of breathtaking beauty and forceful flavour unequalled in any Irish dining room.

A word from the chef

I am not a man of half measures. When I do something, I do it to the best of my ability. And of course I apply these principles to the kitchen.

Cooking, I believe, is about two things; respect and honesty. Respect for the food you handle and honesty to your customers. It is vitally important that the ingredients used are the freshest available. In many ways, I suppose, I have taken this very much for granted. We are lucky enough to have our own garden and farm which supply us with prime vegetables, meat and fresh fish from the river. Knowing where your produce comes from means you can have extra control over the quality of the ingredients and can be assured that they will be fresh and free from additives.

Another thing to bear in mind when you are cooking is the correct seasoning of a dish. My basic rule is to keep it simple; remember, you don't want to lose the original flavour of the dish. One last word of advice: when planning a menu, always look at it as a whole unit and ensure that the different courses complement each other. And above all, enjoy your meal.

William O'Callaghan

MENU 1
Ravioli of Castletownbere Prawns with Courgette Strips
Chicken Consommé scented with Star Anise
Baked Loin of Milk-fed Longueville Lamb
Pyramid of Chocolate and Praline with a Vanilla Sauce

MENU 2
Terrine of Country Pâté
Red Wine Granité
Escalope of Salmon Cooked in Tinfoil
Terrine of Orange and Grapefruit

MENU 3
Gâteau of Provençal Vegetables with a Herb Vinaigrette
Warm Salad of Panfried Scallops and Chopped Chervil
Wild Mallard Duck with Panfried Garden Apples, its Juice Flavoured with Calvados and Vanilla
Tarte Au Chocolat

menu 1

RAVIOLI OF CASTLETOWNBERE PRAWNS

with courgette strips, its juice scented with basil

SERVES 4

12 large prawn tails
1 lb small prawn tails (450 g)
6 large leaves of basil
¼ celery stick
¼ carrot
¼ leek
1 long courgette
2 tomatoes

RAVIOLI DOUGH

7 oz strong flour (200 g)
2 eggs
1 tbsp olive oil
2 egg yolks
zest and juice of 2 lemons (blanch the zests)

SALMON MOUSSE (OPTIONAL)

13 oz fresh salmon (375 g)
1 pint cream (570 ml)
2 egg whites

SALMON MOUSSE

Place the salmon in a food processor and mix with the egg whites.
Pass through a fine sieve.
Refrigerate for ½ an hour.
Then add the cream slowly into the salmon mix and season.

RAVIOLI MIX

Chop the celery, carrot and leek very finely and blanch off in
boiling salted water for 2 minutes and dry.
Chop the basil leaves.
Shell the small prawn tails and chop roughly.
Mix all the ingredients together and refrigerate.

RAVIOLI DOUGH

Place the flour in the food processor. Add the salt and mix.
Add the eggs and egg yolks, juice and zest of lemons and olive oil.
Process until it comes together as a dough.

Wrap in cling film and refrigerate for 1 hour to allow the dough to relax.

LARGE PRAWN TAILS

Blanch in boiling water for 10 seconds and then plunge into iced water. Shell and keep refrigerated until needed.

COURGETTE STRIPS

Using a sharp knife, cut the courgette into ¼ cm wide strips.

TOMATO DICE

Remove the eyes and put into boiling water for 5 seconds and then directly into iced water. It should now be easy to peel the tomatoes. Cut them into quarters, remove the pips and cut them into dice ½ cm square. Keep to one side.

PREPARING THE RAVIOLI

Divide the dough into 8 pieces. Using a pasta machine roll out a piece of dough, sprinkling flour to keep it dry. Roll it out to the second last thickness of the pasta machine.

Make sure that the surface of the machine is kept floured.

Lightly eggwash a strip of dough.

Place ½ teaspoon of the prawn mixture at 2 inch intervals on this strip. When completed cover with a second strip and press the top strip onto the bottom around the mix.

Cut out with a 2 inch cutter

SETTING UP THE PLATE

Place the ravioli into boiling salted water for 4 minutes. Sear off the large prawns in a hot pan and place in the oven for 30 seconds.

Place the courgettes in a casserole and cover with water. Add salt and a basil leaf.

Place on heat and remove once the water has boiled.

Heat the tomatoes quickly in hot water.

Remove the courgette strips and make a round nest shape in the centre of the plate. Place a mound of tomatoes in the centre and three at the edges of the plate.

Place the prawns on the tomato mounds.

Deglaze the pan with bisque or water from courgette saucepan. Whisk in a knob of butter, season and for acidity add a little lemon juice.

Drain the ravioli and place one in the centre and three in between the prawns.

Pour the sauce over the ravioli and prawns and serve.

CHICKEN CONSOMMÉ
scented with star anise

SERVES 8

1 chicken
2 egg whites
1 onion
1 stick of celery
½ clove of garlic
½ bay leaf
1 sprig of thyme
5 black peppercorns
8 star anise (spice available in speciality store)
4 pints of chicken stock (2l 300 ml)

Bone out the chicken breasts and legs.

Remove all skin and fat.

Wash and peel the vegetables and chop up roughly.

Mince the chicken breasts and legs and add in the vegetables, egg whites, herbs, peppercorns and 4 star anise.

Boil the chicken stock and add in the mix, whisking it in vigorously.

When it returns to the boil, reduce to simmer for 20 minutes.

Strain carefully taking care not to upset the mass of solid vegetable and chicken, so that the consommé is absolutely clear.

Season.

TO SERVE: add one star anise.

LOIN OF MILK-FED LONGUEVILLE LAMB

baked with its own juices, lightly scented with parsley & thyme

SERVES 4

1 loin of milk-fed Longueville lamb (12 cutlets)
4 large potatoes, peeled
¼ whole nutmeg
3 tbsp cooking oil

HERB FILLING

1 dsp chopped parsley
1 dsp chopped thyme
clove of garlic
1 ½ dsp olive oil

SAUCE

2 onions
2 carrots
8 tomatoes
1 clove garlic
1 pint veal stock (570 ml)
1 sprig of thyme
1 bay leaf

GARNISH

4 tomatoes
½ tbsp chopped parsley
8 oz spinach (225 g)
½ pint cream (275 ml)

Preheat the oven to 250°C, 500°F, Gas 9.

To prepare the meat, mix together the herb filling ingredients.

Take the loin off the bone leaving the flap intact to the meat.

Remove the fillet. Allow an inch of the flap intact to the meat.

Trim off any excess fat.

Place the fillet beside the thinnest end of the loin.

Rub some of the parsley and thyme mix inside the flap. Season and
fold over onto the meat. Tie up the loin using kitchen string.

Place the roasting tray on a strong heat and allow to get very hot.
Pour in a tablespoon of oil.

Season the loin and brown on the roasting tray, remembering that
you do not want to cook it through, just the outside.

When you have finished, place on a rack somewhere warm,

allowing any fat to drip off.

Then refrigerate for 4-5 hours until the fillet is firm to handle.

Take the string off the fillet and cut into four equal pieces about 4 inches long.

POTATO CRUST

Place a heavy-bottomed pan on the heat with ½ tablespoon of oil.

Place a kitchen cloth on the table and grate the peeled potato onto the cloth.

Season and grate the quarter nutmeg onto the potato. Mix well.

Squeeze out any excess water.

When the pan is hot enough sprinkle the potato mixture onto it and flatten it out with a spoon. Make sure it does not stick to the pan.

Cover with a lid and half cook one side of the potato.

WRAPPING THE LAMB FILLET

Turn the potato mixture onto your worktop, the lesser cooked side up. Cut in half. Put half of the potato onto a light cloth and place the fillet on top. Wrap the potato around the fillet tightly.

GARNISH

Cut the top off the tomatoes so they act as lids. Hollow out the pips and pulp.

Blanch the parsley leaves in a large pot of boiling water for 15 minutes. Chop in a blender, add to the cream and reduce in a heavy-bottomed pan over heat.

Stir regularly so that the bottom of the pan does not burn.

Reduce to a solid consistency.

Take the stems off the spinach and wash three times in cold water to remove sand.

SAUCE

Brown the bones in the oven on a roasting tray.

Add in the vegetables ¾ way through the roasting or when the bones are starting to turn brown.

Place in a large pot and add the herbs, garlic and any stems from the parsley.

Add the veal stock and cover with water. Bring to the boil and simmer for 3 hours.

Pass through a fine sieve and reduce until it is a medium consistency.

COOKING THE MEAT

Colour the potato and fillet in ½ tablespoon of oil in a
heavy-bottomed pan. Place in a hot oven and cook for 15 minutes,
turning the fillet 3-4 times.

Heat the sauce and season. Heat the parsley purée and season.
Place the tomatoes in the oven until cooked, and season them. Melt
3 oz butter in a heavy-bottomed pot and cook the spinach in it
stirring at regular intervals. This will take a little time.
Test when cooked.

TO SERVE: Strain the spinach and divide amongst four plates,
placing it in the centre. Fill the tomato with the parsley purée and
place on the spinach. When the lamb is cooked rose pink, divide it
in three and place around the plate. Check the sauce again and you
may add a little of the parsley and thyme mix.

If you wish, adjust for acidity with lemon juice. Pour the sauce over
the fillet slices and serve.

PYRAMID OF CHOCOLATE & PRALINE

with a vanilla sauce

SERVES 8-12

VANILLA SAUCE

10 egg yolks
I ¾ pt milk (1 litre)
4 vanilla pods
5 oz castor sugar (150 g)
7 fl oz cream (200 ml)
13 oz dark chocolate melted in bain marie (375 g)

PRALINE

9 oz almond (250 g)
9 oz sugar (250 g)
1 oz glucose syrup (25g)
5 oz butter (150 g)
4 fl oz Tia Maria liqueur (125 ml)

You need to make the pyramid-shaped moulds first. They consist of
three triangular cardboard cut-outs, 4 inches x 4 inches x 4 inches,
which you stick together to form the pyramid. Line with plastic.
Heat the milk and cream with the vanilla pods and keep aside to
infuse.

Cream the egg yolks and the sugar, strain the milk and pour onto the yolks.

Return to the pan and cook till the custard coats the back of the spoon. Allow to cool.

Caramelise the sugar and syrup and stir in the almonds. Allow to cool. Liquidise in the food processor.

Add 9/10 of the vanilla sauce, the Tia Maria, cool melted butter, cool melted chocolate and fold in the whipped cream gently. Pour into the pyramid moulds and place in the freezer.

TO SERVE: Remove the pyramids from the moulds. Pour some of the remaining vanilla sauce onto each plate and place a pyramid in the centre. Garnish with black cherries, orange zest and a sprig of mint.

menu 2
TERRINE OF COUNTRY PÂTÉ
SERVES 8

1 lb pork meat trimmings (450 g)
1 lb pork fat (450 g)
grated nutmeg
1 dsp freshly chopped parsley

MARINADE

1 glass white wine
1 tbsp brandy
½ onion, chopped
1 bay leaf
1 sprig of thyme (leaves only)
1 sprig of rosemary (leaves only)
2 lb loaf tin

Mix all the ingredients for the marinade with the pig fat and pig trimmings and leave to marinate in the fridge for three days.

On the third day turn on your oven to a very low temperature, about 150°C, 300°F , Gas 4.

Mince the marinated ingredients (not too finely), add in the marinade and then grate the nutmeg into the mix.

The mix should be quite moist so add more white wine if needed.

Season the mix more than you think it needs as it will lose it during cooking, about 1 tsp pepper and 2 tsp salt.

Mix in well and fill your terrine mould with the mixture.
Place in a bain marie and cook in the oven for about three hours.
Rest it for 2 days before eating.

RED WINE GRANITÉ
SERVES 6

1 bottle red wine
4 oz sugar (110 g)

Heat up the red wine with the sugar until the sugar has melted.
Once it has come to the boil, remove.
Place in a mixing bowl in the freezer and whisk the mixture every
half hour once it starts to freeze. Alternatively, place in an icecream
maker until frozen.
TO SERVE: Serve in a well chilled wine glass.

ESCALOPE OF SALMON
cooked in tinfoil

SERVES 4

4 thick escalopes of salmon
4 handfuls of well-washed spinach (1lb/450 g)
4 medium sized carrots
4 leeks
4 courgettes (zucchini)
4 sprigs tarragon
4 knobs of butter
1 tbsp lemon juice
salt and pepper
16 fl oz fish stock (440 ml)

Preheat the oven to 250°C, 500°F, Gas 9.
Peel the carrots and cut into three-inch pieces.
Wash the courgettes and cut into three-inch pieces, discarding the
top and bottom.
With a knife cut the leeks (from just above the roots) up through the
middle of the plant. Wash the leek and cut into three-inch pieces.
Using a sharp chopping knife, chop the vegetables lengthways into
twice the width of a matchstick.
Heat up a frying pan and sweat off the chopped vegetables using a
knob of butter.

Cook them until they are half cooked.

Take 4 lengths of tinfoil about 3 feet long and fold in two.

On each one, place some raw spinach in the middle of one half with the sweated vegetables on top.

Season.

Season the escalopes of salmon on both sides and lay them on top of the vegetables.

Place a sprig of tarragon on top of the salmon.

Mix the lemon juice with the fish stock and season.

Fold the top half of the tinfoil over the half which contains the fish and vegetables.

Seal the edges all the way around, leaving just a hole at the end to pour in the fish stock.

When the fish stock has been added finish sealing the parcel.

When you want to cook the fish, gently transfer it onto a baking tray and heat up the tray on top of the stove so that the parcel expands and inflates. This should take a minute or two. Then place the parcels in a hot oven for six minutes.

Serve as quickly as possible so that the parcel does not deflate.

Cut the tinfoil open in front of the person being served so that they can smell the beautiful aroma.

TO SERVE: Serve on a hot plate the same way as you placed it in the tinfoil.

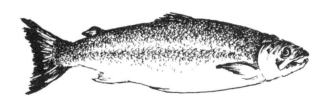

TERRINE OF ORANGE & GRAPEFRUIT

SERVES 8

5 oranges
5 grapefruit
5 pink grapefruit

JELLY

4 fl oz fresh orange juice (100 ml)
4 fl oz sweet white wine (100 ml)
4 ½ sheets of gelatine (generous ½ oz/12 g powdered gelatine)
1 vanilla pod
3 oz sugar (75 g)
5 pink peppercorns
6 fresh mint leaves
1 fl oz passion fruit juice, approximately 4 passion fruit (25 ml)
2 lb loaf tin

Segment the oranges and grapefruit and keep aside any orange
juice (to make jelly).

Boil the orange juice, wine, vanilla, sugar, pink peppercorns, mint
and passion fruit juice together.

Then add the gelatine and let the mixture cool down, stirring from
time to time. Pour a little of the jelly mixture into the terrine mould,
just enough to cover the bottom of the mould.

Then add a layer of oranges, followed by a little jelly, a layer of
grapefruit, a little more jelly and a layer of pink grapefruit.

Keep following this procedure until you reach the top of the terrine.
Allow the jelly to set.

(Always add just a little jelly, if you add too much it will be too
rubbery.)

TO SERVE: Briefly immerse the terrine mould in a basin of very hot
water. This will loosen the sides and allow you to tip it out onto a
serving dish. Make sure the serving dish is slightly wet so that you
can move the terrine around to position it in the centre.

NOTE: To make passion fruit juice, scoop out the pulp and seeds and press through a sieve.

Loin of Milk-fed Longueville Lamb, see page 66

Ravioli of Castletownbere Prawns, see page 63

Pyramid of Chocolate and Praline, see page 68

The Presidents' Dining Room at Longueville House

The Drawing Room at Longueville House

Traditional Roast Duck with Sage and Onion Stuffing, see page 90

Apple Vol au Vents, see page 91

Courtyard Setting, Ballymaloe House

The Conservatory at Ballymaloe House

Quail Stuffed with Chicken Mousseline, see page 101

Pineapple and Strawberry Timbale, see page 104

The Staircase Gallery at Newport House

menu 3

GÂTEAU OF PROVENÇAL VEGETABLES
with herb vinaigrette

SERVES 4

knob of butter
salt and freshly ground black pepper
fresh herbs to garnish
1 red, 1 green and 1 yellow pepper
4 handfuls spinach (1lb/450 g)
1 aubergine (approx 3 inch diameter)
1 small clove of garlic
1 large courgette
2 lbs tomatoes (900 g)
4 tbsp olive oil
1 small onion, chopped
1 garlic clove, crushed
a little grated orange zest
10 fl oz olive oil (275 ml)
4 basil leaves, finely chopped
1 sprig of thyme and rosemary
1 garlic clove, crushed
¼ tbsp white wine vinegar
a pinch of salt

Preheat the oven to 240°C, 475°F, Gas 9.

Butter a baking tray lightly.

Halve the peppers lengthwise and put them on the baking tray in the oven.

Bake for about 9 minutes.

Remove from the oven.

Boil the spinach and strain well to remove the juices.

Cook the garlic in the butter and add to the spinach.

This mixture should be quite dry. Allow to cool.

Blanch the peppers in boiling water for 1 minute. Skin them and then dice the flesh finely.

Fry briefly in a tablespoon of olive oil, then drain on absorbent paper, season and leave to cool.

Reduce the oven temperature to 180°C, 350°F, Gas 4.

Cut the aubergine crosswise into four 1 inch round slices.

Fry gently on both sides in 2 tablespoons of olive oil, then place on a wire rack in the oven until soft, about 10 minutes.

Remove, and drain on absorbent paper, season and leave to cool. Slice the courgettes into circles of coin thickness. Fry off in a tablespoon of olive oil, then drain on absorbent paper and leave to cool.

Put the tomatoes in boiling water for 10 seconds, then drain, skin, remove the seeds and dice the flesh.

Fry the onion and garlic in the remaining oil until soft, then add the tomato and orange zest and stir-fry briefly.

Line four ramekins tightly with aluminium foil. Place the aubergine slices in the bottom of each, then overlap the courgette slices around the ramekin, each slice resting half on the aubergine, half up the sides of the ramekin. Add 1 tablespoon of the tomato mixture to the centre, top with spinach. Then cover with another tablespoon of tomato. Top off with some of the pepper dice.

For the vinaigrette, heat the olive oil gently with the herbs and garlic. Whisk the remaining ingredients, add salt and pepper and a cup of water, then whisk into the oil. Strain.

TO SERVE: Place a little vinaigrette on each plate. Unmould the gâteau and place in the centre of the plate with little mounds of pepper dice and herbs.

WARM SALAD OF PANFRIED SCALLOPS
and chopped chervil

SERVES 4

6 large scallops in shell
4 handfuls of lettuce leaves using a selection of the following,
oakleaf, buttercup, frisse, mash and lolo rosso
1 bunch chervil
10 sorrel leaves
1 tsp chopped chives
2 tsp chopped chervil
2 tsp hazelnut oil
1 dsp balsamic vinegar

Fill the sink full of cold water.

Carefully prepare the lettuce by discarding the outer dead leaves and larger old leaves into a bowl.

Cut off all the nice fresh leaves into the water.

Toss the leaves twice in the water so as not to bruise them.

Fill a lettuce spinner ¾ full of lettuce and turn twice, discarding water each time.

Place in a box with a cold wet towel underneath and cover the lettuce. Keep refrigerated.

Remove the scallops from the shells and separate the coral.

Wash off any sand. Dry the scallops and season them.

Sear them in a heavy bottomed saucepan with a dessertspoon of olive oil.

Do not cook the centre.

Mix the salad, chopped chives and a teaspoon of chopped chervil.

Season with salt and pepper. Add 2 teaspoons of hazelnut oil and 1 dessertspoon of balsamic vinegar.

Taste to check.

Dress the plate, placing the scallops around the salad (in the centre).

Deglaze the pan with 2 tablespoons of water. Whisk in a knob of butter and chopped chervil.

Season with salt, pepper and a drop of lemon juice.

TO SERVE: Pour the sauce over the scallops and serve.

WILD MALLARD DUCK
with panfried garden apples, its juice flavoured with Calvados and vanilla

SERVES 4

2 wild mallard ducks
12 apples (Cox's Orange Pippins, if possible)
16 fl oz veal stock (250 ml)
16 fl oz chicken stock (250 ml)
16 fl oz water (250 ml)
4 tbsp Calvados
½ vanilla pod
seasonings

When the duck has been cleaned and singed, remove the collar bone, neck, the two legs and the back of the duck.

Keep the two breasts to one side and chop the remainder.

Place on a roasting tray with a tablespoon of oil.

Colour on top of the stove for five minutes and then finish browning them in the oven.

While the carcasses are browning, cut the apples into eighths, cutting down through the centre.

Turn each piece into a barrel shape and keep the trimmings for the sauce.

When the bones are brown place them in a casserole.

Pour the fat off the roasting tray and deglaze the tray with Calvados.

Reduce it and add in the two stocks and water.

Simmer for 5 minutes and pour it into the casserole with the bones.

Add the apple trimmings and vanilla.

Simmer for 20 minutes and then pass through a fine sieve.

Reduce the sauce by boiling it if it is too thin.

Place a heavy-bottomed pan on the stove and heat it up.

Pour in a tablespoon of oil and colour the breasts of duck.

Then place them in a hot oven at 250°C, 500°F, Gas 9.

Cook the duck for 10-12 minutes until it is pink.

Do not overcook, so utmost care is needed at this point.

When cooked let it rest on a tray in a warm place for at least 5 minutes.

Meanwhile, heat up a heavy-bottomed, sufficiently wide-rimmed pan or casserole until it is very hot and add a teaspoon of oil.

Then add in the apples and cover well.

They can be deglazed with a drop of Calvados just before taking them off.

Remove the skin, and the layer of fat under the skin, from the duck breasts.

Slice the skin, sprinkle with a pinch of salt and grill.

Keep to one side.

Slice the breasts and arrange on the plate.

Place the apples at the top of the plate with the grilled skin.

Pour the heated sauce around the duck and serve.

TARTE AU CHOCOLAT
SERVES 6

BUTTER FOR FILLING

5 oz bitter chocolate couverture/dark chocolate (150 g)
1 egg
2 egg yolks
1 oz sugar (30 g)
4 oz butter (100g)

CHOCOLATE SWEET PASTE

8 oz flour (325 g)
4 oz cocoa (125 g)
7 oz icing sugar (190 g)
3 oz almonds (70 g)
12 oz butter (300 g)
1 ½ eggs
5g salt
7 inch flan tin

CHOCOLATE SWEET PASTE

Preheat the oven to 200°C, 400°F, Gas 6.

Sieve the flour, cocoa and icing sugar, add to the ground almonds.
Rub in the butter.

Add the eggs and salt, and knead together. Chill in the fridge for 2 hours.

Roll out and line the flan tin.

Prick the bottom with a fork and bake blind in a hot oven for 10 minutes.

FILLING

Bring the butter to room temperature and cut into small pieces.

Carefully melt the chocolate in a bain marie.

In a machine, whisk together the eggs and sugar to a white ribbon, and slowly add the softened butter.

Add in the melted chocolate and pour onto the pastry case. Cook for 25 minutes at 180°C, 350°F, Gas 4. Serve hot.

NOTE: This pastry is difficult to make and quite crumbly. Work together quickly and chill well. If it is difficult to roll out, use the palms of your hands. However, short crust pastry could be used instead, but substitute 1 oz of cocoa powder for 1 oz of flour.

Ballymaloe

SHANAGARRY, CO. CORK

*I*n the late 1940s Ivan Allen, a fruit farmer, and his young wife Myrtle were looking for a larger farm. Ballymaloe House with its 400 acres came up at auction. And there being no other bids, the Allens bought it. It was a house they had both known for many years - indeed they had actually met at a dinner party there. Myrtle had always been a keen cook and in 1964, encouraged by her husband, she opened a small restaurant in the dining room of the house. Two years later they opened three bedrooms for paying guests.

Now they have thirty bedrooms and an international reputation; supermarkets stock Ballymaloe pickles; one daughter runs a restaurant in Cork city, another has an excellent shop in the yard beside the house, selling everything from spices to sweaters; one son runs the farm which provides almost all the ingredients for the culinary operations, a daughter-in-law has a cookery school just down the road. Ivan is the wine expert and is responsible for bringing together the list of interesting and reasonably priced wines. With six children and their spouses and twenty

grandchildren, almost all of whom are involved in the business in some way, Myrtle and Ivan have founded a dynasty that Caesar himself would have been proud of.

Although originally a castle of the Fitzgeralds, you will not find baronial grandeur at Ballymaloe. It is far more a rambling old country house, a family home filled with unexpected delights and charming corners. Between the battlemented tower on the west side and the sixteenth-century gatehouse to the east, is what looks at first like a simple late Georgian home, until you realise that the castle wall divides it down the middle, and a seventeenth-century stronghouse sprouts from one end. Inside the rooms are simply furnished but hung with a superb and immensely important collection of contemporary Irish art collected by Ivan Allen.

Ballymaloe has a wonderfully friendly and happy atmosphere. No demands of formality are made on the guests and there can be few more welcoming families than the Allens.

A word from the chef

It is hard to imagine, now, how remote and isolated country house living was for the first fifty or sixty years of this century. There was almost no prepared food in the village shops beyond tinned salmon and sardines, peas and baked beans. There was, however, plenty of good fresh food in the fields, gardens, dairies and little butchers' shops, so on country house tables, when a good cook took charge, one could eat the finest food in Ireland.

Here are three seasonal menus using these traditional ingredients:

Autumn. From early September, through to the first severe frost, watercress is at its best. Cook it briefly to retain its bright green colour. Fat ducklings with a fresh sage stuffing are in season, as also are Beauty of Bath or Worcester Permain apples, for a more sophisticated sweet.

Spring. Mussels and citrus fruit are at their best during the early spring months. It is often difficult to find all the fruit for the salad at one time. It will not matter if some of them are omitted or the quantities changed slightly. The starter and sweet can be made in advance and the tournedos do not take long to cook at the last minute.

Summer. A cool, light starter is best with the rich but simple lobster dish which is finished at the last minute. Freshly picked blackcurrants make a delicious icecream.

Myrtle Allen

Myrtle Allen

MENU 1

Watercress Soup
Traditional Roast Duck with Sage and Onion Stuffing
Apple Vol Au Vents

MENU 2

Grape, Grapefruit and Mint Cocktail
Hot Buttered Lobster
Blackcurrant Icecream

MENU 3

Mussel Soup
Tournedos Steaks with Mushrooms
Citrus Fruit Salad
Petit Fours Chocolate, Nut and Raisin Clusters

menu 1
WATERCRESS SOUP

SERVES 4

2 oz butter (50 g)
4 oz chopped onions (110 g)
5 oz chopped potatoes (150 g)
8 oz chopped watercress (225 g)
1 pint water (570 ml)
¾ pint milk (425 ml)
1 egg yolk
1 tbsp thick cream
salt and pepper

GARNISH

2 tbsp whipped cream, watercress leaves

Melt the butter in a heavy-bottomed pot.
Add the onions and potatoes, stir until well coated. Season with salt and pepper, cover with a butter paper and a tight-fitting lid.
Sweat on a very low flame for 10 minutes, taking care not to brown.
Add the water and boil for a few minutes until the vegetables are quite soft.
Add the watercress and boil one minute more.

Remove from the heat and purée the soup.

Re-heat, add the milk, taste and adjust seasoning.

Just before serving add the egg yolk beaten into the cream.

Do not boil again.

TO SERVE: Garnish with whipped cream and watercress leaves.

TRADITIONAL ROAST DUCK
with sage and onion stuffing, gravy and apple sauce

SERVES 4

Allow one 4 lb duck for 4 people

TO MAKE STOCK FOR GRAVY

duck neck, wing tips, heart and gizzard
1 small sliced carrot
1 small sliced onion
bouquet garni

Put the duck pieces into a small saucepan with the herbs and vegetables.

Cover with cold water and a lid, and leave to simmer slowly for 20 minutes.

Strain through a sieve lined with muslin.

STUFFING

1 ½ oz butter (40 g)
3 oz chopped onion (75 g)
1 round tbsp freshly chopped sage
4 oz breadcrumbs (110 g)
salt and pepper

Heat the butter, add the onion and cook for about 5 minutes, or until softened.

Remove from the heat, and stir in the sage, breadcrumbs, salt and pepper to taste.

TO PREPARE AND COOK DUCK

Preheat the oven to 200°C, 400°F, Gas 6.

Wash and dry the duck.

Season the duck cavity with salt and pepper.

Spoon the stuffing into the cavity.

Season the breast.

Roast, breast side up, for 20 minutes approximately.

Reduce the heat to 180°C, 350°F, Gas 4 for approx 45 minutes more, or until the juices run clear when thigh is pricked.

Transfer the duck to a serving dish; spoon excess fat from the roasting pan.

Add the stock to the pan, bring the liquid to the boil, stirring to scrape up the brown bits, and cook it over a moderate heat for a few minutes more, or until the gravy is thickened slightly.

Season to taste with salt and pepper.

APPLE SAUCE

½ lb cooking apples (225 g)
2 fl oz water (55 ml)
4 oz sugar (110 g)

Peel and core the apples; cut into chunks.

Cook with the sugar and water on a low heat in a covered pot until soft.

Purée or serve just as it is, as preferred.

TO SERVE: Serve the gravy and apple sauce separately.

APPLE VOL AU VENTS
SERVES 4

APPLE FILLING

4 small eating apples - use Beauty of Bath, Worcester Permain or Cox's Orange Pippins
3 oz castor sugar (75 g)
½ lemon
1 ½ tbsp Irish Mist

Peel, quarter and cut the apples into ⅛ inch thick (3mm) slices.

Put them in a stainless steel or enamelled saucepan.

Add the sugar and juice of a lemon.

Cover the pan tightly and cook on a gentle heat until the apples are soft but not broken. Stir in the Irish Mist.

FOR PASTRY CREAM

6 fl oz milk (175 ml)
vanilla pod or vanilla essence
2 egg yolks
1 egg white
2 oz sugar (50 g)
½ oz flour (10 g)

Bring the milk to the boil with a small piece of vanilla pod in it or add a few drops of vanilla essence afterwards.

Separate the yolks and whites of the eggs.

Beat the yolks together and pour the boiling milk onto them.

Beat in the sugar and the sifted flour.

Stir on a very low heat, until the custard is thick and cooked.

Use a heavy-bottomed saucepan, and be careful to prevent sticking or lumps forming.

Strain into a clean bowl.

Beat the egg whites stiffly and fold them in. Cool.

FOR CASES

¾ lb puff pastry (350 g)

Roll out the pastry ¼ inch (5 mm) thick.

Stamp out into 3 inch (7.5 cm) rounds.

They will shrink by about ½ inch diameter when cooked.

Mark the centre by half-cutting with a 1 ½ inch (4 cm) cutter.

Bake in a hot oven, 240°C, 475°F, Gas 9, until risen and browned.

Cool, remove lids and scrape out the soft pastry from inside.

TO MAKE UP

5 oz whipped cream (150 ml)
prepared ingredients
Irish Mist or Calvados
icing sugar

Mix ½ pint (275 ml) of pastry cream with whipped cream, stir in the apple juices to flavour and liqueur if desired.

Fill the pastry cases ⅔ full with this mixture and pile the apples on top.

Put the lids on and dredge heavily with icing sugar.

TO SERVE: Serve within an hour if possible.

menu 2
GRAPE, GRAPEFRUIT & MINT COCKTAIL
SERVES 4

2 grapefruit
8 oz seedless grapes, peeled (225 g)
1 tsp finely chopped mint
sugar to taste

Cut the grapefruit segments carefully from the surrounding membrane.

Scrape out the remainder of the juice and membrane from the grapefruit skin and add the strained juice to the segments.

Add the mint, grapes, and sugar if necessary.

Fill back into the skins and chill.

HOT BUTTERED LOBSTER
SERVES 4

4 x 1lb lobster (450 g)
6 oz butter (175 g)
1 lemon

Kill and lightly cook the lobster.

Split it open and remove the sac.

Put the meat from the body, tail and claws and all green juices into a warm bowl wrapped in a tea-towel.

Heat the lobster shells.

Melt the butter in a frying pan.

When foaming, toss the lobster in it until the meat is cooked through and the green juices have turned red; use plenty of butter and do not overcrowd the pan.

Spoon the meat back into the hot shells.

Put the rest of the butter into the pan, heat and scrape up any remaining bits.

Pour into a hot sauce-boat or individual heated butter dishes.

TO SERVE: Serve with quartered lemon, green salad and brown bread.

BROWN SODA BREAD

1 lb wholemeal flour (450 g)
7 oz white plain flour (200 g)
2 oz oatmeal (50 g)
1 rounded tsp bread soda
1 rounded tsp salt
1 pt buttermilk (570 ml)

Preheat the oven to 200°C, 400°F, Gas 6.

Mix the dry ingredients together. Make a dip in the middle and pour in all the milk at once.

Stir gently until evenly moistened, working as little as possible. Do not knead.

Sprinkle a little flour on a baking sheet and turn out the dough on it. Sprinkle with a little more flour and flatten into a round cake.

Cut the traditional deep cross on top.

Bake for 45-50 minutes approximately.

BLACKCURRANT ICECREAM

SERVES 4

3 ½ oz sugar (90 g)
4 fl oz water (125 ml)
5 oz blackcurrants, strings removed (150 g)
1 oz sugar (25 g)
2 fl oz water (55 ml)
1 egg yolk
½ pint whipped cream (275 ml)

Combine 3 ½ oz sugar (90 g) with 4 fl oz water (125 ml).

Bring to the boil and add the blackcurrants and bring back to the boil again.

Remove from the heat, purée and cool.

Boil the remaining 1 oz sugar (25g) and 2 fl oz water (55 ml).

It will look thick and syrupy and when a metal spoon is dipped in, the last drops of syrup will form thin threads.

Beat this a little at a time into the egg yolks, continuing until it becomes a thick creamy white mousse.

Fold in the cream and cooked purée.

Freeze.

menu 3

MUSSEL SOUP
SERVES 4

3 lb mussels (1 kg 350 g)
8 fl oz dry white wine (225 ml)
5 tbsp finely chopped shallots or spring onions
½ clove garlic, crushed
small bunch parsley
½ bay leaf
1 sprig thyme
1 oz butter (25 g)
1 oz flour (25 g)
1 egg yolk
2 fl oz cream (55 ml)
milk for thinning
1 oz butter (25 g)

FOR GARNISH

1 rounded tbsp finely chopped parsley
2 rounded tbsp diced croutons, fried until brown

Wash the mussels in cold water, remove the beards and scrape clean if necessary.

In a non-aluminium saucepan heat together the wine, shallots or spring onions, garlic and herbs.

Add the mussels and stir over heat until the shells open.

Remove from the pot and take half the mussels out of their shells, saving the juices.

Discard the empty shells.

Keep the mussels aside but return all juices to the saucepan.

Boil down for a minute or two.

Melt in 1 oz butter (25 g), stir in the flour, cook over a moderate heat, stirring for 2 minutes.

Strain in the mussel liquid and bring to the boil, whisking out any lumps that may form.

In a bowl blend the egg yolk with the cream.

Pour in the boiled soup, whisking as you go.

Return to the saucepan and boil up again.

Taste and add the milk until you get a good flavour and consistency.

Just before serving add the shelled mussels, beat in the remaining butter and sprinkle with chopped parsley and croutons.

TOURNEDOS STEAKS WITH MUSHROOMS

SERVES 4

8 slices of bread
8 tournedos steaks, 1 inch thick (2.5 cm),
tied into neat mounds with string
2 oz diced streaky bacon (50 g)
2 oz finely chopped shallot or spring onion (50 g)
10 fl oz red wine (275 ml)
10 fl oz stock (275 ml)
9 oz sliced button mushrooms (250 g)
½ oz chicken liver pâté (10 g)

All the frying is done in a mixture of oil and butter, using minimum quantities.

Cut the bread into rounds to fit the tournedos.

Fry the bacon and shallot together until cooked, 5 minutes approximately.

Add the red wine and stock.

Reduce by half and put aside for the sauce.

Sauté the mushrooms for a minute.

Add them with their juices to the sauce.

Fry the bread until golden on both sides. Keep warm.

Season the tournedos and cook in a teaspoon each of hot butter and oil.

Allow 2 minutes per side for medium rare and 3 minutes for well done.

Place the tournedos on top of the croutons and keep warm.

Pour the reserved sauce into the pan in which they were fried.

Boil down to about 5 fl oz liquid (150 ml), scraping the pan.

Stir in the pâté.

Pour over the steaks and serve immediately.

There should not be very much sauce, but it should have thickened and be very full of flavour.

CITRUS FRUIT SALAD
SERVES 4

1 oz sugar (25 g)
2 oz kumquats (50 g)
2 small clementines
1 satsuma
1 blood orange
½ large jaffa orange
½ large pink grapefruit
juice of one lime
ugli fruit and pomelos as available

Dissolve the sugar in 2 fl oz water (55 ml), and bring to the boil.
Add the thinly sliced kumquats and poach until softened.
Peel the satsuma and cut into rings.
Peel the clementines and divide into segments.
Cut away the peel and pith of the blood orange, jaffa orange and grapefruit, then cut the segments out from the surrounding membranes.
Add the satsuma and clementines to the kumquats.
Stir in the lime juice to taste and segments of pomelo and ugli fruit, if available.
Serve chilled.

PETIT FOURS CHOCOLATE, NUT & RAISIN CLUSTERS *makes approx. 10 chocolates*

3 heaped tbsp raisins
1 heaped tbsp hazelnuts, skinned and roasted
3 oz chocolate (75 g)

Melt the chocolate in a bowl suspended over a saucepan of boiling water.
Mix in the fruit and nuts and put out in teaspoonsful piled onto greaseproof paper or into petit four cases.
Leave to cool and set.

Newport

NEWPORT, CO. MAYO

*C*lew Bay is a place of magic and legend - the magic of 365 islands, the legends of Grace O'Malley, pirate Queen of Connaught. The magic of Owen Cullen's way with fish, who has managed the Newport fishery since 1945, and the legends of the fish not caught - fifty pounds and fighting like a tiger! The magic of the setting Atlantic sun on Newport House's crimson, creeper-clad Georgian façade and the legends of the O'Donnell clan, descendants of the Earls of Tyreconnell, who lived there for 200 years.

Nearly half a century has passed since Henry Mumford-Smith took on Newport House and converted it into a hotel. Now Kieran and Thelma Thompson carry on the tradition, having bought the house in 1985. The comments of the "Signpost Guide", published in 1949, are still accurate. "A gracious country house with a kindly welcome. Food noted for its skilful preparation and pleasant presentation. Of the amenities one should note good plumbing."

The house, though built on the site of an early castle, dates from 1720.

In the late Regency period an imposing wing was added with an enormous dining room and, above it, an equally impressive drawing room. The two sections of the house are linked by an elegant galleried staircase hall, worthy of "Gone With The Wind". When it was built there were, of course, no handy supermarkets and the estate had to be totally self-sufficient for all its food. Two hundred and fifty years later the kitchens are still supplied with fresh produce from the fishery, garden and farm.

History is alive at Newport. Apart from the various medieval abbeys and ruined castles in the area, a Psalter written by St. Columcille around A.D. 650 was discovered in the library of the house (it is now in the Royal Irish Academy). Just down the road is the megalithic tomb where the lovers Diarmuid and Grainne were overtaken by Fionn Mac Cumhaill and beyond it is the island of Innisdaff, which has a reputation for ghostly apparitions.

Ten miles away in Westport a street market is held every Thursday, where herbs and vegetables from the Smiths' farm and farmhouse cheeses such as Carrowholly and Cuilmore Blue are available. And at Rosbeg, Patrick Percival acts as a broker for the "rare foods" that are produced in the area. Newport is certainly a place to feed both body and soul, and with 16 loughs in the area as well as 8 miles of its own river fishing, pure paradise for anglers.

A word from the chef

We believe that the single most important factor in good cooking is the quality of the basic ingredients. We are fortunate at Newport House in having access to excellent local produce. Salmon from our own river and lake, sea fish straight from the boats in Achill, excellent local beef and lamb, and vegetables and herbs from our own gardens. With produce of this quality one has only to allow the natural flavours to emerge by delicate cooking, employing sauces which complement, rather than cloak, the natural flavours.

Cooking fish is very much a case in point. The less you do to it the better - it is so easy to ruin good fish by over-cooking and over-seasoning. A sauce is often necessary, but we feel it should be delicately complementary. We have included three quite straightforward fish dishes. The first uses salmon which is panfried gently and served with a light sorrel sauce. The natural flavour of the salmon dominates and its richness is delicately offset by the tartness of the sauce.

In our second menu, we start with feather-light quenelles of fish. The important thing to remember when making the quenelles is to let the mixture chill thoroughly before folding in the cream. John Dory, which has a marvellously delicate flavour and texture, is featured as the main course. It is served encrusted with slivers of potato which you must cut through to savour the fish.

Our third menu is more a winter menu. Rilettes of duck are followed by excellent venison cooked in a wild mushroom and game sauce. We finish off with an old favourite, bread and butter pudding, which is totally transformed served with whiskey sauce.

John Gavin

John Gavin

MENU 1

Quail stuffed with Chicken Mousseline with a Tarragon Sauce
Carrot and Coriander Soup
Wild Salmon with Sorrel Sauce
Pineapple and Strawberry Timbale

MENU 2

Quenelles of Salmon, Turbot and Monkfish with a Carrot and Lime Sauce
Green Salad with Walnut Oil Dressing
John Dory with Potato Crust and Champagne Sauce
Summer Pudding

MENU 3

Rillette of Duck
Leek and Potato Soup
Medallions of Venison with Wild Mushroom and Game Sauce
Bread and Butter Pudding with Whiskey Sauce

menu 1

QUAIL STUFFED WITH CHICKEN MOUSSELINE *with a tarragon sauce*

SERVES 4

MOUSSELINE OF CHICKEN

5 oz chicken breast (150 g)
12 fl oz cream (360 ml)
salt and pepper
1 tbsp tarragon

Mix the chicken in a food processor, then leave in a cold room/fridge to cool off.

When the chicken is cool turn the processor on and slowly add the cream.

Season with salt and pepper.

Then add the chopped tarragon.

QUAIL

4 quail
1 oz butter (25 g)
salt and pepper

Preheat the oven to 220°C, 425°F, Gas 7.

Cut a line down through the middle of the quail breast flesh.

Ease the meat off on both sides.

Remove the breast bone from the quail and keep for stock.

Fill the quail with the mousseline and keep together with cocktail sticks.

Season and seal on a hot buttered pan.

Cook for 7-10 minutes in your preheated oven.

When cooked split in two and serve with tarragon sauce.

TARRAGON SAUCE

1 sprig tarragon
1 ½ glasses dry white wine
½ glass brandy
½ pint good chicken stock (275 ml)
1 oz butter (25 g)
1 tsp chopped tarragon
1 tsp chopped shallots
bones from quails
2-3 tbsp cream

Melt the butter in a pan; add the quail bones and chopped shallots.

Sauté for 5 minutes, without colouring.

Add in the white wine and reduce by half.

Add the brandy and chicken stock.

Reduce by ⅔ and strain through a fine sieve.

Season with salt and pepper, and add cream to correct consistency.

CARROT AND CORIANDER SOUP
SERVES 4

½ lb carrots (225 g)
1 oz onions (25 g)
1 oz celery (25 g)
1 oz leek (25 g)
½ oz butter (10 g)
1 ½ pint chicken stock (850 ml)
1 dsp chopped chives
salt and pepper
coriander to taste

Melt the butter in a saucepan, add the roughly chopped vegetables.

Cook without colour for 5-7 minutes with the lid on.

Add the chicken stock and simmer for ½ hour.

Liquidise.

Pass through a fine strainer.

Season with salt, pepper and coriander to taste.

Sprinkle with chopped chives.

WILD SALMON
with sorrel sauce

SERVES 4

4 salmon fillets
juice of 1 lime
salt and pepper

Season the salmon fillets with salt, pepper and lime juice.

Lightly butter a non-stick frying pan, heat, then put on the salmon fillets and fry for ½ minute on each side to seal without colour.

Brush with melted butter then place under the grill for ½ minute only.

The salmon should be barely cooked through.

SORREL SAUCE

1 pint fish stock (570 ml)
½ glass vermouth
½ glass white wine
¼ pint cream (150 ml)
2 oz sorrel (50 g)
juice of 1 lemon
2 oz chopped shallots (50 g)
½ oz butter (10 g)

Melt the butter in a pan.

Add the vermouth, white wine and chopped shallots.

Reduce by two-thirds.

Add the cream, lemon juice and season.

Reduce to coating consistency.

Strain, and add the shredded sorrel.

TO SERVE: Serve on a hot plate with the sorrel sauce and garnished with a tomato rose.

PINEAPPLE & STRAWBERRY TIMBALE
with vanilla sauce, icecream and caramel cages

SERVES 4

4 pineapple rings
1 punnet strawberries

Arrange the pineapple rings in the centre of each plate. Surround them with sliced strawberries and pour vanilla sauce around the fruit.

Dot the sauce in 6 or 7 places with a raspberry coulis and run a knife through to form hearts (optional).

Place a scoop of banana and rum ice-cream in the centre of the pineapple ring and place a caramel cage over.

VANILLA SAUCE

6 egg yolks
3 oz sugar (75g)
1 pint milk (570 ml)
½ vanilla pod

Heat the milk with the vanilla pod. Remove the pod after a few minutes.

In a bowl combine the egg yolks and sugar with a balloon whisk, and slowly add the vanilla-flavoured milk. When all the milk has been added return to the saucepan and proceed to heat the mixture until it coats the spoon lightly. Do not allow to boil.

BANANA AND RUM ICECREAM

2 eggs
3 oz castor sugar (75 g)
3 tbsp honey
2 medium sized bananas, mashed
3 tbsp dark rum
18 fl oz cream (½ litre)
9 fl oz milk (¼ litre)
juice of half a lemon

In a large bowl, beat the eggs until blended.
Beat in the sugar and honey until smooth and light.
Stir in the bananas and lemon juice.
Stir in the milk, cream and rum.
Pour into an icecream machine and leave running until the mixture is frozen.

CARAMEL CAGES

3 ½ fl oz water (90 ml)
7 oz castor sugar (200 g)

In a heavy saucepan, dissolve the sugar in water over a gentle heat and allow to continue cooking until the mixture is just starting to turn golden.

Remove from the heat and cool for about 1 minute until it begins to harden.

Make your trellis by using the back of a greased soup ladle as a mould - dip a spoon into the caramel and pull the thread back and forth, forming a cage.

Carefully twist the cage free and place on a tray.

Repeat the process by reheating the caramel in the pan.

menu 2

QUENELLES OF SALMON, TURBOT & MONKFISH *with carrot and lime sauce*

SERVES 4

SALMON QUENELLE

5 oz skinned fresh salmon (150 g)
½ egg white
4 fl oz cream (110 ml)
salt and pepper
¼ tsp fresh dill

TURBOT QUENELLE

5 oz skinned fresh turbot (150 g)
½ egg white
4 fl oz cream (110 ml)
salt and pepper

MONKFISH QUENELLE

5 oz fresh fillet of monkfish (150 g)
½ egg white
4 fl oz cream (110 ml)
salt and pepper
¼ tsp fresh basil

Roughly chop the salmon and purée in a food processor with dill, salt and pepper. While the machine is running add the egg white. Transfer to a mixing bowl and chill in a refrigerator for 45 minutes. Slowly mix in the cold cream, and correct the seasoning. Proceed as above to make the turbot and monkfish mousse.

Three-quarters fill a large saucepan with seasoned fish stock, bring to the boil and simmer. Using two warm tablespoons, form the mousse mixture into quenelles (egg shape) and poach for about 4 minutes.

CARROT AND LIME SAUCE

¼ lb carrots (110 g)
10 fl oz fish stock (275 ml)
½ oz chopped shallots (10 g)
½ oz butter (10 g)
4 fl oz white wine (110 ml)
2 tbsp cream
juice of 1 lime
salt and pepper

Sweat the shallots in the butter, add the carrots, white wine and fish stock and cook until the carrots are soft.

Add the lime juice and liquidise. Pass through a fine sieve. Add the cream and season with salt and pepper.

TO SERVE: Divide the sauce between 4 plates and place three quenelles - one of each mousse - on each plate. Garnish with a carrot rose and fresh basil.

NOTE: At home one could make just one type of fish mousse and triple the quantities.

GREEN SALAD
with walnut oil dressing

SERVES 6

½ *head oakleaf lettuce*
½ *head radichio*
½ *head lolo rosso*
½ *head frisse lettuce*

Pick the lettuce into bite size pieces.
Wash thoroughly and dry in a salad spinner.

DRESSING

6 fl oz vegetable oil (190 ml)
3 fl oz walnut oil (75 ml)
3 fl oz white wine vinegar (75 ml)
1 oz Dijon mustard (25 g)
1 oz English mustard (25 g)
salt and pepper (approx 5g each)
2 parsley stalks
2 shallots, sliced

Mix the mustard, vinegar, salt, pepper, oils, shallots and parsley.
Allow to marinate overnight and then strain.

JOHN DORY
with potato crust and champagne sauce

SERVES 4

4 small fillets of John Dory
7 oz potatoes (200 g)
1 egg yolk
pinch flour
1 oz butter (25 g)

Peel, wash and cut the potatoes into fine strips. Heat the butter in a non-stick pan and add the potatoes, stirring continuously.
Cook for 2-3 minutes.
Drain in a colander.
When drained place in a bowl, add the egg yolk and season with salt and pepper.
Lightly flour the fillets of John Dory.
Season liberally and spread some of the potato mixture on top.
Place in the refrigerator until set and ready for cooking.

CHAMPAGNE SAUCE

1 oz butter (25 g)
2 oz mushrooms (50 g)
2 oz shallots (50 g)
5 fl oz dry sparkling wine (150 ml)
5 fl oz cream (150 ml)
5 fl oz fish stock (150 ml)

Melt the butter, add the mushrooms and shallots (thinly sliced) and sweat until soft.
Add the wine and reduce by half.
Add the cream and cook until slightly thickened.
Season to taste.
Pan fry the fish with the potato side down first.
Once browned, turn over and cook for a further 3 minutes.
When cooked place on absorbent paper.
TO SERVE: On individual plates, place a serving of fish and pour some of the sauce around it.

SUMMER PUDDING
SERVES 4-6

8 -10 slices of bread (crusts removed)
6 oz strawberries (175 g)
6 oz raspberries (175 g)
6 oz loganberries (175 g)
6 oz blackcurrants (175 g)

SYRUP

6 fl oz water (180 ml)
7 oz sugar (200 g)
juice of 1 lemon
8 whole cloves
pinch mixed spice
pinch cinnamon

Cut the slices of bread into fingers and line the pudding dish, reserving the remaining bread fingers.

Place the fruit into the boiling syrup and simmer for 10 minutes, then allow to cool.

Pour into the pudding dish, and cover with the remaining bread. Pour the liquid from the fruit over the pudding.

Press down with a weight and allow to rest for 12 hours in the refrigerator.

RASPBERRY SAUCE

9 oz raspberries (250 g)
3 ¼ oz castor sugar (80 g)
juice of 1 lemon

Sieve the raspberries and stir in the sugar and lemon.

TO SERVE: Turn out the summer pudding and surround with the raspberry sauce. Decorate with fresh fruit.

menu 3

RILLETTE OF DUCK
SERVES 4

4 duck legs
2 tbsp duck fat (lard)
1 carrot
1 leek
2 sticks celery
1 onion
10 juniper berries
1 tbsp ginger
1 tbsp marjoram

FOR GARNISHING

1 red pepper
¼ pint mayonnaise (150 ml)
6 green peppercorns, crushed

Preheat the oven to 170°C, 325°F, Gas 3.

On a preheated roasting tray, melt the duck fat or lard.

Add the roughly chopped vegetables.

Place the duck legs on top, add seasonings and spices.

Cover with aluminium foil and cook at a very low temperature for 2 - 2 ½ hours or until the duck meat flakes away from the bone.

When cooked, flake the meat from the bone and chop roughly.

Add a fine dice of pepper and green peppercorns.

Bind with the mayonnaise and refrigerate for up to 2 hours.

Using 2 dessertspoons, shape into quenelles and place on the plate.

Bring to room temperature and serve with garlic croutons.

TO SERVE: Serve with a small salad dressed with mustard vinaigrette.

LEEK AND POTATO SOUP
SERVES 4-6

4 leeks
2 oz butter (50 g)
4 oz onions (110 g)
3 oz celery (75 g)
8-10 oz potatoes (225-275g)
2 pints white stock (1l 150 ml)
¼ pint cream (150 ml)
sprig thyme and sage
salt and pepper

Cut and peel the washed mixed vegetables and cook slowly, without colouring, in melted butter.
Add the stock, sliced potatoes, thyme and sage.
Simmer until the vegetables are tender.
Liquidise, season with salt and pepper and pass through a fine sieve.
Reheat and finally add cream.

MEDALLIONS OF VENISON
with wild mushroom and game sauce

SERVES 4

8 x 3 oz medallions of venison (75 g)
3 chopped shallots
2 oz butter (50 g)
8 oz mixed wild mushrooms (225 g)
3 oz button mushrooms (75 g)
1 tbsp brandy
2 tbsp Madeira
¾ pint game stock (425 ml)
sprigs of parsley
salt and pepper

Season the medallions and sauté in butter until pink.
Remove the medallions, put the chopped shallots into the pan, and cook without colouring.
Add the mushrooms, and sweat for 3-4 minutes.
Add the brandy, Madeira and game stock - allow to reduce by ⅓.
Add the cream. Bring to the boil, season with salt and pepper.
TO SERVE: Serve the medallions covered with sauce and garnished with parsley.

BREAD AND BUTTER PUDDING
with whiskey sauce

SERVES 4

½ pint milk (275 ml)
½ pint cream (275 ml)
2 whole eggs
2 oz sultanas (50 g)
3 oz castor sugar (75 g)
1 tbsp vanilla essence
12 slices white bread, toasted
2 oz butter (50 g)

Preheat the oven to 150°C, 300°F, Gas 2.
Cut the toast with a 2 inch round cutter.
Butter, then layer into 4 lightly greased ramekins, alternating with
the washed sultanas.
Whisk the eggs and sugar, add the milk and cream and pass
through a fine strainer into each ramekin.
Stand in a roasting tin half-full of water and cook in a moderate
oven for between 45 minutes to 1 hour.

WHISKEY SAUCE

4 oz castor sugar (110 g)
5 oz butter (150 g)
1 whole egg
1 ½ measures whiskey

Melt the butter in a saucepan, and add the castor sugar.
When the sugar is dissolved take off the heat and add the egg,
whisking vigorously, then add the whiskey.
TO SERVE: Turn out the bread and butter pudding onto 4 plates.
Pour the whiskey sauce over the top.